W9-AHP-566

Study Ab...

A Manual for A...

50 0560831 7

Study Abroad

A Manual for Asian Students

BRIGID BALLARD and JOHN CLANCHY

Longman

LONGMAN MALAYSIA SDN. BHD.
3, Jalan Kilang A, 46050 Petaling Jaya, Selangor Darul Ehsan.
Tel: 03-7920466, 7920803

Associated companies, branches and representatives
throughout the world.

First published 1984
Reprinted 1988, 1990, 1991, 1992, 1993 (twice), 1995 (twice), 1996

ISBN 0 582 72429 5

Study Abroad A Manual for Asian Students

Text set in 10/12 pt. Times Roman
Printed by Percetakan Anda Sdn.Bhd., Seri Petaling, Kuala Lumpur.

Preface

We have written *Study Abroad* because, in our work with under-graduates and postgraduates at the Australian National University, we meet many overseas students who have encountered unexpected problems with their studies. Before coming overseas these students expected they would have difficulty with English, especially academic written English; and, almost invariably, they do. In fact so obvious are their problems with language that both academic staff and the students themselves tend initially to explain away all of their problems as 'difficulties with English'. But we think this stereotype is misleading. It is just as misleading as that other explanation which would attribute all difficulties to 'homesickness' and 'culture shock', though these too are very real problems and ones which are also anticipated before departure.

There is, in our experience, a more fundamental problem for overseas students which is both unanticipated by them and seldom recognized by staff. Students are surprised to find that they must make significant shifts in

- their approach to study,
- their styles of learning, and
- their ways of developing arguments and presenting ideas.

These shifts are intellectual, rather than linguistic or social. They require a change from previous methods, which have worked well enough at another level of education and in another culture, to a new approach which is seldom made explicit by staff or set down in study guides. Such changes may be more disconcerting for post-graduates than for undergraduates, and for students in Arts and Social Science Faculties than for those in Science and Engineering. The shift will probably be greater for students from some Asian cultures than from others, and for students to whom English is a foreign language than for those who have been at least partly educated in the medium of English. It is with this problem of adjustment in styles of thinking and study — rather than simply with English or social orientation — that we are concerned in this book.

We anticipate that this book will be of use to four types of reader. First, we have in mind the individual student in Asia who is planning to study abroad and who wishes to prepare for this future. The very fact that this student is attempting self-help is already a step in the direction of independent and critical learning, which is the focus of much of the book. Second, we anticipate the book will be used by groups of students, in language training or orientation courses, who are being more systematically prepared for study overseas. We have, therefore, included practical exercises which should stimulate discussion in such a setting. Third, we expect it will be useful for students who are already enrolled in a foreign university and have run into unexpected problems in their study. Finally, we hope it will be illuminating for the teachers of such students, whether in their home country or abroad.

In writing this book we have drawn on our many years of experience in working with tertiary students in Australia and other parts of the world. We have also benefited from a three-month study tour of some Southeast Asian countries, meeting academic and secondary school teachers and students in order to learn something of the educational and cultural traditions which Asian students bring with them when they go abroad to study. Finally, and most importantly, we have learned much from our own students from Asia who, over the years, have come to us with their study problems, have filled in our tedious questionnaires, have fed us with their excellent cooking, and have courteously brought us to recognize our own cultural and intellectual blinkers. If this book is of use to Asian students, it is largely because of what we have learned from their predecessors — and we are grateful to them.

Contents

POSTGRADUATE STUDIES

APPENDICES

Introduction

Dear Student,

We have written this book to help you prepare yourself for your university or college studies·abroad. There are many books and courses which offer you help in improving your English. There are others which prepare you for some of the day-by-day problems you will meet when you live in a foreign country. Here, however, we are concerned mostly with the changes you will need to make in your study habits and in the way you develop and present your ideas.

You may be surprised that any changes in your study methods are necessary — after all, you are already a successful student in your own school or university system. Yet, in our experience, many students from overseas, and especially from Asia, do have real problems in adjusting to the intellectual culture of universities in Australia, Britain and elsewhere in the English speaking world. They have problems in the following areas:

- understanding how the university or college system works,
- making effective use of all the resources of the university or college they attend,
- understanding the relationship between academic staff and students, and recognizing what is expected of students by their lecturers,
- discarding, or transforming, approaches to study which are no longer appropriate,
- studying and learning with increasing independence, and
- learning to think critically and argue systematically.

In this book we shall discuss all of these points. We have included many comments by Asian students who have studied in Australia, for their experience will be close to your own. We have based much of our discussion on experience in Australian universities, because we ourselves work there, but the points we explore are common to all western tertiary systems. Where there are significant differences between national systems, we have added Appendices to cover information for Britain, Canada and the United States. We have not drawn comparisons between these systems and those you know in your own country — that is for you to do, either on your own or in discussion with other students. You may find the exercises at the end of each chapter are useful starting points for making such comparisons.

How to use this book

When you use this book we suggest that you may find it helpful first just to glance through it quickly, and then read the sections that concern you most. But do not stop there. As you will soon realize, each section of the book depends on information and ideas developed in other sections. If you want to know what will be expected of you as an undergraduate, you will find it useful to read about the secondary school background of your fellow students. Similarly, if you are a postgraduate, it will be important to know the system in which other research students have been educated as undergraduates. So, though you may start with the section that most immediately applies to you, you will probably find yourself working gradually through the whole book, fitting together the ideas and explanations like pieces of a jigsaw puzzle in order to get a complete picture.

Two of the chapters — Chapters 2 and 5 — are more theoretical than the others. In Chapter 2 we try to demonstrate the differences that exist between cultures in styles of thinking and presenting ideas. In Chapter 5 we explain in detail the process of critical thinking which underlies tertiary study in a western education system. You may find it useful to read the more practical chapters first, looking at the specific strategies for effective study, and then go back to these two general chapters as a way of reflecting on these strategies.

At the end of each chapter there is a section 'More to think about'. Here you will find three exercises which develop ideas raised in the chapter. Although you can do all of these exercises independently, the first in each set is specially designed for individual work, the second can lead to co-operative work and discussion with another student, and the third can be used as a class exercise.

There are no Golden Rules which guarantee successful study but throughout this book we have emphasized the useful sequence of **observe**, **practise**, and **participate**. **Observe** what experienced students do; **practise** these skills for yourself; and then **use** them in your own studies.

So now you are ready to start.

We hope this book will be useful to you while you are planning and preparing to go abroad for further studies. We think you will also find it helpful when you arrive at your new college or university and are beginning to meet some of the problems we have discussed here. Above all, we hope that this book will help you to succeed in your studies overseas so that you both obtain the qualification you want and gain the greatest benefit from your training abroad.

Brigid A. Ballard

John Manchy

Acknowledgements

We are grateful to the following for permission to reproduce copyright material:

The University of California Press for an extract from *To Make My Name Good* by P. Drucker and R. Heizer on pages 55–58 and Blackwell Scientific Publications Limited for an extract from 'Habitat Selection' by Linda Patridge in *Behavioural Ecology* (ed. Krebs & Davies) on pages 124–126.

We also wish to thank all the teachers and students in Australia and Asia who have contributed in so many different ways to the creation of this book.

Chapter 1
The Problems of Studying Abroad

If you are hoping to go abroad to study, what are the main problems you expect to find? New foods? Making friends? Problems with English? Homesickness? If you talk with people who have come back from study abroad, they will tell you that they had difficulties with at least some of these things. They will also encourage you by telling you of some of the good things they experienced: the places they've visited and the people they've met, and perhaps the well-equipped libraries or laboratories in which they've worked.

Then, if they are talking with you seriously, they will probably start telling you about the **unexpected** problems they found with their studies: the different atmosphere of a foreign university, the different attitudes of lecturers and students towards study and research, the need to adjust their old study habits to new ways of working.

In this book we will be looking mainly at the way in which you will need to change your approaches to study in order to work successfully in a university or college overseas. Of course difficulties with language, with differences between cultures, and with living far away from home and friends are also important. But these are problems you are already aware of. The problems in adapting to a new style of learning are probably unexpected — but they are real. A Bangladesh undergraduate called them 'Study Shock'.

1 Language problems

In our experience nearly all foreign students who come to Australia to study have problems with English. In a survey of the difficulties overseas students at the Australian National University (ANU) encountered in their studies, problems with English were the most frequently mentioned. Listen to some of their comments:

> I can still remember when I first came here, the main problem was understanding what people were saying. It's true that we learn English

in Hong Kong, but learning English is very different from communicating in English. People here speak English with a very heavy Australian accent which makes it even harder to understand and besides, they speak very fast too.

(Hong Kong undergraduate in Science)

When I first started my course in ANU the main problem is that I did not understand the lectures (it's my language problem). I have difficulties in following lectures and lab demonstration, in using the library or technical equipment, in discussing my work with supervisors or lecturers, in organizing an essay, in taking part in tutorials. Sometimes my problem is I know the subject and meaning in my language but I don't know how to explain and write the assignment in English. (Always using my Burmese dictionary made my head ache.) I understand the main point is I must try harder than the other students because English is my second language, but the language problem made me depressed.

(Burmese undergraduate in Science)

The most essential problem is language (English). It is the problem both in following the class and the tutorials, and in doing general assignments including essays, and in communicating with the people. I am sure I will enjoy my course more and more if I can cope with this problem well. Other problems may well be handled when I can understand what the Australians say and I can make them understand what I am talking about.

(Thai undergraduate in Arts)

Then another major problem which I experienced (even until now) is the English language. It's a great obstacle as· at times I find it really hard to converse fluently in English; even though my secondary education was conducted in English, there was little need for me to speak English — I studied in English but yet I conversed in our own exotic mother tongue (ironic, isn't it). That's why Asian students are rather quiet during tutorials and lectures as they are afraid that with their low command of spoken English it will be embarrassing.

(Malaysian undergraduate in Economics)

The language problem is very real. Yet, as you may have noticed when you were reading those comments by Asian students, this is much more of a problem at the start of your course. It usually becomes less serious after a few months of living and working in surroundings where English is spoken all the time and where all reading and writing are also in English. Gradually you become 'acclimatized' to English.

Before you go abroad you will probably enrol in special English courses. Some of these may help you with English conversation. In others you will work particularly on grammar and vocabulary. You will probably take a course preparing you for English tests which you must pass before you can be accepted by a college or university in an English-speaking country. Also in order to practise your English you will probably try to do some extra reading in English and, maybe, seek out people who speak English. In these ways you will already be helping yourself to overcome the problem of language.

Nevertheless you will almost certainly have an initial difficulty with English when you begin your studies. As a Singapore postgraduate commented: 'Preparatory classes do help a bit but they only have limited use as the standard required for academic study is high.' A Korean scientist put her view even more strongly:

> When I couldn't express myself, what I try to explain, what I have in mind, what ideas I have about my research, then I feel I have become a fool. This language problem deprives me of my confidence in my study sometimes.

But don't despair. At your university or college there will be people ready to help you with your English. Some institutions have a special Language Centre where English is taught to both overseas students and to new migrants. Some have special counsellors or tutors who can help you. In others there are schemes by which students help each other. There are often organizations which arrange visits by overseas students to local families. And there are usually language laboratories, books and other facilities in the university or college which you can use in your spare time.

So English will certainly be a problem but one that you can gradually overcome. After all, most students have problems with expressing themselves clearly — even in their own language.

2 Living abroad

A second problem you must expect to meet is the difficulty of living in another culture, far away from home, family and friends. Asian students who have studied abroad talk of their loneliness there and refer to it as part of 'the price' of an overseas qualification. This cost, of course, has to be balanced against the positive aspects of the experience. But it is a cost which has to be borne.

To some extent, again, you can prepare yourself in advance by finding out as much as you can about the country, the city, and the university or college to which you are going. You may be able to attend an orientation course before you leave home. You can seek out people who have returned from study abroad and learn from

their experiences. There are practical things you can learn to do. If
you know, for example, that you are going to have to cook for yourself or that there are certain dishes which you really enjoy, then get
someone at home to teach you how to cook. Many of your fellow
students overseas will be only too willing to exchange language lessons for a meal of chicken biryani or a dish of nasi goreng.

On arrival at your college you will probably find there are already
students there from your own country who will be ready to help you
settle in. A Malaysian Law student made the point:

> I suggest that a good way of building up confidence is by talking to
> other Asians (oldies). They are the people who can give really good
> tips as they too had to undergo the same problems at the beginning.

Also many colleges have special organizations for overseas students
to help them meet other students and make new friends.

Here are the comments of two more Asian undergraduates:

> Adaptation to life here was the first acute problem that I encountered
> when I just landed here in ANU in March 1980. Everything was just
> not right; food, friends, weather, you name it — everything was a
> problem then. To add to my misery any homesickness, the weather
> was of no help, especially during the winter when I really get miser-
> able. Then luckily things made a good turn for me as I started to find
> my way around and started to win precious friendship. And as the
> time passed by I realized that adaptation was not that hard as I had
> just thought. Guess what! I could not even eat raw lettuce, tomatoes,
> not to mention the exotic spaghetti and pizza, when I first came, but
> now don't mention it — I could eat a horse. Food here is not as good as
> food back home, but to survive we have got to learn not to be choosy
> and ultimately to love some, if not most, of the food here now.

> I had more problems in first year at ANU than I have now and most
> of these are related more to relationships with Australian and other
> overseas students rather than my studies. After having spent a year in
> Melbourne where I mixed a lot with overseas students, I found I had
> difficulties (1) adjusting to uni. work, (2) mixing more with Western-
> ers than Asians, (3) with the climate (boy! was it cold that first win-
> ter). Finding some good trustworthy friends is most important to me
> and if I can't confide in someone to give vent to my frustrations and
> loneliness, it affects other areas of my life, especially my work. Need-
> less to say, being far away from home, etc. tends to increase my frus-
> trations. I might add here that I'm not saying I find Westerners (esp.
> Australians) unfriendly, untrustworthy, etc. but I can't change the
> fact that I am a Malaysian Chinese and there are some things that
> non-Malaysian Chinese can't understand when I say 'I ache here or
> there'.

Judging from the experiences of these and other overseas students, you too are going to meet many expected and unexpected problems in your daily life: problems of loneliness, of finance, of climate, and of correct behaviour. Yet these are all part of the 'education' you have come to seek. And there will always be fellow students and other people ready to help you.

3 Adapting to new study patterns

The third area of difficulty, the problems in adjusting to a new style of teaching and learning, is less likely to be discussed before your departure from your own country. You yourself may not expect any serious difficulties in this area. After all you have already proved, in the long years of your schooling, that you are an outstanding student. Otherwise you would not have qualified to study for a degree abroad. Probably you have always been successful in your studies, and you have developed a pattern of studying which has worked very well in the past.

Yet listen to these students describing their experience of studying abroad:

Problems that I am facing now are:

(1) Note taking in lectures. I find it hard to both listen, absorb and write at the same time. Very often, I find I don't quite get what the lecturer is trying to convey at the instant he finishes his sentence and the next moment, he's going on to something else. I do feel sometimes I'm more a recording machine (trying to write down most of the things the lecturer said) than trying to get the essence of the lecture.

(2) Reading. I guess preparing lectures would help in understanding the lectures, however, to understand what the book is trying to say is also a problem. I have to spend a long time to read a page and sometimes I have to read it more than once to understand what the paragraphs mean.

(3) Laboratory work. I did not find it such a problem because it was what I know at home. But it was hard sometimes to understand what is meant in the lab manuals. And the lab staff seem to speak too fast for me. They think I know more than I really do about where to find things and how to set things up.

(4) Writing essays. It is a new experience for me to look up relevant materials from the large variety of books in the library. I very often don't know where to start from. Research work is very time consuming. The understanding of the question/essay too is a bit of a problem. Luckily, this can be remedied by asking tutors concerned.

(*Hong Kong undergraduate in Science/Economics*)

I had a serious problem in writing essays in social science. Since my BA was in English Literature, I was not trained to argue something in essays. So my essays tended to be very descriptive and my argument was weak. In tutorials, it was difficult to see the break of discussion at the beginning. So although I wanted to speak up, I could not start speaking and was so frustrated.

(Japanese postgraduate in Soc. Science)

In my first year because of a lack of basic vocabulary I had some difficulties in following lectures, as well as in taking notes. I had no idea how to take notes for a start, and I didn't know how to handle time-table and leisure time. It took rather a long time to get used to the libraries and when I asked the staff behind the inquiry desk I was never sure if I got what he meant. There was very little contact between I and my classmates in a big hall where the lectures were taking place. I was very slow in reading and writing. Meanwhile I doubted if my own notes could be of any use and was anxious about how to catch up with others most time. When it's necessary to speak to the lecturers or tutors, I was conscious of my own awkward way in expressing myself, and was worried about assessment and final marks from an early time. There always were problems in essay writing and in understanding what our teachers' expectations were.

(Chinese undergraduate in Asian Studies)

So it seems that you will need to be ready to change your habits of study as well as cope with the obvious problems with language and living in a foreign country. These changes will be necessary because of the different 'culture' of the new education system. There may be new tasks which you must perform. You may have to write long essays or lab reports — in English. You may have to go to the library and work independently on the books and journals there. You may have to design and carry out lab experiments. You may be expected to present a paper in a seminar or join in a tutorial discussion.

These tasks assume that you are capable of working independently, of using lectures or textbooks as a starting point for further reading and thinking, and that you will approach your studies with a critical and questioning mind. This approach may be new to you. It is, to some degree, a new approach for all students coming from secondary school. At school you are expected to memorize and accept the information provided by your teacher or the textbook. At college or university you are encouraged to analyse and question information drawn from a wide variety of sources.

In the rest of this book we shall be mainly examining this new approach to learning. We shall also give you a general introduction to the structure of degrees and some understanding of what academic staff expect of their students. Finally we shall suggest practical strategies for success in both undergraduate and postgraduate levels of study. We believe that, although competence in English and ease in a new cultural setting are certainly important, managing this shift to a new style of thinking and working is probably your most important step towards gaining a degree in a Western university system.

Summary

In this chapter we have looked at some of the problems which students meet when they go abroad to study.

Two common and **expected** problems are:

- lack of fluency in English both for conversation and for academic purposes, and
- coping with living in a foreign culture.

An **unexpected** but very important problem is:

- the need to change habits of thinking, studying and learning to suit the demands of the foreign education system.

It is this last problem which we deal with intensively in the rest of this book.

MORE TO THINK ABOUT

1 Think about the changes in study habits you have had to make during your education up to the present:
   - when you moved from primary to secondary school, what changes were you required to make in the way you studied?
   - if you have studied at university in your own country, what further changes did you have to make when you moved from secondary to tertiary level study?

Make a list of the most important changes you have made.

On the basis of what you have read in this chapter, what **additional** changes will be necessary when you go abroad to study?

2 Imagine that you have been asked to write some background information for a student who is coming to study in your country.

List, with brief explanations, the five most important things you think this student should know in order to prepare for studying in your own university, college or school.

Discuss your list with a fellow student and work out a combined list.

3 Interview someone who has returned from study abroad about the difficulties he or she met. You might find it helpful to base your questions on the headings we have used in this chapter: **Language, Daily Life,** and **Study Habits**. Find out how this person coped with those difficulties. Make notes on the interview and discuss these with other members of your class.

(Alternatively, you might invite one or more returned students to give a brief talk to your class and then answer your questions.)

Chapter 2
Cultural Variations in Styles of Thinking

1 What do we mean by 'cultural variations' in styles of thinking?

Is it true that people from different cultures 'think differently'? Are
some styles of thinking more suited to certain tasks and certain contexts than others?

These are complicated questions which lead to much academic
argument. What does seem clear from our experience is that students from different cultures often bring different **purposes** to their
thinking and learning. And these different purposes produce different results, for example in the way the students respond to an essay
topic, a problem or a controversial piece of research. The following
description of a Japanese undergraduate's essay may help to explain
what we mean by different purposes producing different results.

A Japanese student, who had studied Economics successfully for
two years in Tokyo before coming to Australia, came to seek help
after he had failed all his first semester Economics courses in our
university. His English was weak and he was very shy. He explained
that he had difficulty in keeping up with the reading for his courses,
so he had relied on reading his old Japanese textbooks rather than
struggling with the English language books prescribed in the course.
He also felt extremely nervous in tutorials and so never spoke. He
had not completed any of the optional assignments because he
either did not have enough time or else felt his attempts were so
poor that he was ashamed to hand them in. He failed all his mid-
year exams, partly because of the difficulty in understanding the
complex language of the questions. So here was a student whose
attempt to adapt to Australian university study had been a failure.

At the beginning of the second semester he came to us for help
with this essay question for Economic History:

> Compare Friedman's views of economic planning in postwar Europe
> with those of Samuelson.

The lecturer's purpose in setting this topic was to lead students to
compare the views of Friedman and Samuelson, that is to analyse

the significant similarities and differences between these views, and then **evaluate** them. The Japanese student, however, took a very different approach. He began by describing, in detail, the family background and personal life of Friedman up to the time he published his economic analysis of postwar Europe. The points of this analysis were summarized briefly, without comment. Exactly the same information was given about Samuelson. And there the essay ended.

This essay would probably be criticized by an Australian lecturer in these terms: 'What is the relevance of all this information?'; 'You have not made any attempt to **analyse** or **compare** the two approaches'; 'What is your **conclusion** about the relative merits of each man's views?'; 'What **evidence** have you found to support either set of views?'. And the lecturer might dismiss this student as unpromising because there were no signs in the essay that he could do more than summarize information — no sign, in short, of **critical thinking**.

When we discussed this essay draft, however, it became clear that the student had very deliberately organized his thinking and writing according to the way he had been trained to write essays in Japan. His aim in writing about Friedman and Samuelson was not to point out the strengths and weaknesses of their economic thinking (critical analysis). Rather, his purpose was to create for the reader a harmonious understanding of the reasons why two eminent economists could reach conflicting judgements on economic planning. By describing the difference in their backgrounds, he was implicitly explaining how these conflicting viewpoints developed. So his 'Japanese' purpose was very different from the 'Australian' purpose intended by the lecturer.

The form of the essay was also different, as it lacked any conclusion which might have summarized the main points made in the body of the essay. In Japan, the student explained, he would not be expected to put forward his own critical evaluation of a controversy between eminent scholars. So once again the reason for this difference in the essay was not incompetence but a difference in cultural style. It would not be correct, he had been taught, to write a conclusion which tells the reader what he should think; that would be bad manners — a student should not impose his own views on his lecturer.

This student, therefore, was writing his essay according to a clear academic style appropriate within his own Japanese culture. Yet an Australian lecturer, judging the essay in terms of his own cultural style, would not find it acceptable. So the student had to learn to adjust his purpose and to adapt the structure of his essay to meet the expectations of his lecturer. Once he was able to see that the problem was not a matter of English or of knowledge about the two economists but of **the way in which he was approaching the whole essay task**, then he was able to make the necessary shifts without any great difficulty. And by the end of the year this student was regularly receiving Credit grades for his essays. His written English was still often incorrect but one of his lecturers commented: 'He is a promising student because he shows he can think clearly, even though he still has problems with formal English'. So this Japanese student had now made a successful shift to the style of 'thinking' required by his Australian lecturers. He had made the crucial adjustment.

2 Cultural attitudes to learning

As we can see from the case of our Japanese student, most students think and study and write in the way they have been trained at school and university. Each country has its own traditions not only about **what** a student must learn but also **how** he should learn. In some countries students are not encouraged to ask questions; in other countries they are expected to question both their teachers and the materials they are learning. In some countries the teacher or lecturer provides all the information which the students must learn; in others students are expected to find most of their material independently, by reading or by their own experiments and research. When a student trained in one cultural tradition moves, as you are planning to move, to study in another country, a different style of learning is often necessary.

Look at Figure 1 on page 12 which sets out some characteristics of different attitudes to knowledge and learning. These differences lead to variations in ways of studying.

All of the characteristics presented in this diagram can be found in all education systems and in all cultures. Some learning strategies, however, are given more importance than others according to the **context** in which they occur. It is the context that determines which learning strategy is preferred. We can see, for example, how this applies to different levels of schooling in the Australian education system. In primary and secondary school, to a large extent, students learn by memorizing information, solving problems and following procedures set by the teacher. We have called this the **reproductive** approach to learning. The move to tertiary education, in particular to university education, involves an important shift to a new approach to learning — the **analytical** approach. In this context students are required not simply to memorize but to question and think critically about the knowledge that is presented to them. And,

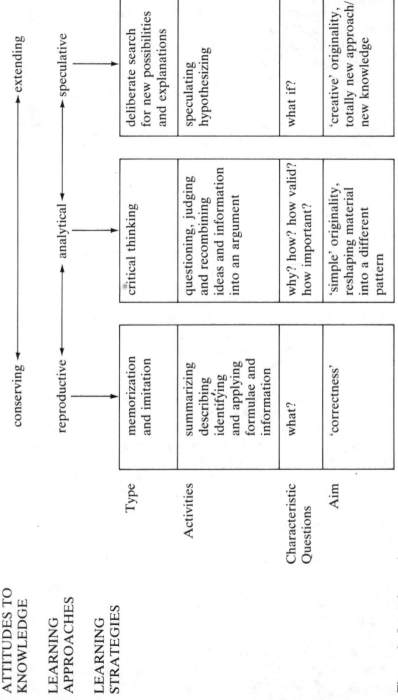

ATTITUDES TO KNOWLEDGE	conserving ←——————————→ extending		
LEARNING APPROACHES	reproductive ←→ analytical ←→ speculative		
LEARNING STRATEGIES			
Type	memorization and imitation	critical thinking	deliberate search for new possibilities and explanations
Activities	summarizing describing identifying and applying formulae and information	questioning, judging and recombining ideas and information into an argument	speculating hypothesizing
Characteristic Questions	what?	why? how? how valid? how important?	what if?
Aim	'correctness'	'simple' originality, reshaping material into a different pattern	'creative' originality, totally new approach/ new knowledge

Figure 1: Learning styles

gradually, university students are encouraged to move on to the third approach: to **speculate** and to develop independent research, which is the purpose of postgraduate and advanced studies.

Of course these learning styles are never totally separate at any stage: in school the more senior students will probably be asked to think critically as well as to memorize, to do some independent reading as well as copy teachers' notes from the board. And at university, particularly in science and mathematics, there will be times when students must learn facts and formulae by heart, as well as developing their critical judgement by analysing, questioning and evaluating the information and results they are working on.

Are there other contexts — apart from the level of education — in which certain learning strategies are preferred over others? Do some cultures, for example, tend to value questioning and criticizing more highly than others? Are there cultures in which the emphasis in education given to preserving traditional knowledge (the **conserving** attitude) is very much greater than that given to testing and questioning that knowledge (the **extending** attitude)? And if so, what difficulties face the student who moves from one culture to another?

Consider these comments by three Asian students who found the Australian university system of teaching and learning very different from their previous experience:

Studies: generally, many of us are trained in a system where you don't contribute much to class discussions, some even hesitated to ask questions from lecturers. One must do it properly, i.e. fully conscious and forever calculating to ask questions or not. Here you are encouraged to ask anything that bothers you. This drawback is related to our culture of respect to others, especially the elderly and the better qualified — but it inhibits the fullest development of oneself. In my country there is no 'openness' of discussion and learning.

(Singapore undergraduate)

Also in Japanese culture (and education) the emphasis on training seems to be on intuition rather than logical construction of argument. This made it much harder for me to explain what I want to say in essays or in tutorials.

(Japanese MA student)

One problem was getting used to the system where a student is expected to find out for her/himself the requirements and facilities of the University. This contrasts with the system at home whereby a person, generally the lecturer/supervisor, is responsible to the needs of the student . . . Also logical approaches are different. For example, in order to answer a question by a straight yes/no, there is a tendency to go around the point (circumlocution) which probably stems from the influence of the home language.

(*Indian PhD student*)

Another way of understanding the problems a student from another culture may face in moving to a Western university system is to consider the case of an Indonesian postgraduate student who was writing her thesis on Indonesian literature. Her first attempt at writing the opening chapters of her thesis was severely criticized by her supervisor because it was 'merely descriptive'. In the first chapter the student had recounted the personal life of the author she was studying. Her next chapter consisted of a detailed summary, with long quotations, of a short story he had written. The next chapter was a summary of a novel, and so on. Her supervisor complained: 'This work is not up to the level of senior high school students. It is disastrous for a student at postgraduate level.' Yet, as the student explained, her approach to literary criticism was exactly the style used in her own country and the tradition in which she had been trained. The job of the literary critic, she explained, is to make the life and works of an author available and understandable to a wider public; the way to do this is to summarize the author's writings.

Once this student began to read critical articles written by Western literary critics, she could recognize that her approach must change. Gradually she developed the capacity — and the courage — to question, to analyse and to develop critical views about the works of her author. And her thesis was successful. Looking back on this slow process of change she commented: 'Now I am beginning to see what I must do. I am learning how to ask questions. And which questions to ask. Before I didn't even know there were any questions at all, did I?'

3 Cultural influences on styles of writing and presenting ideas

So there do seem to be ways of approaching knowledge and study which are given more emphasis in some cultures than in others, and in some subjects, or disciplines, than in others. There seem also to be distinctive styles of writing and organizing ideas which reflect these differences.

Robert Kaplan, an American, drew attention to 'the cultural differences in the nature of rhetoric' based on his analysis of the written work of overseas students studying in his Los Angeles university.[1] He argues that different cultures produce distinctive

[1] Robert B. Kaplan, 'Cultural Thought Patterns in Inter-cultural Education', *Language Learning*, 16 (1966): 1–20

approaches to thinking and writing, just as they each have a distinctive language. He suggests that it is a fallacy to assume that 'because a student can write an adequate essay in his native language he can necessarily write an adequate essay in a second language'. Briefly, he supports his view by analysis of the students' writing. He claims that there are at least five distinct patterns for structuring an 'expository' paragraph — a paragraph that is developing ideas rather than telling a story. Within Western cultures, for example, he distinguishes the English pattern which he calls linear, i.e. moving directly from the central idea to explanations and examples, from Romance and Russian patterns which permit some movement away from the central idea. In the English pattern such divergence would break the rules of relevance. Kaplan also identifies a Semitic pattern, covering the Arabic and related cultural traditions, which emphasizes the development of an idea through parallelism: a statement is made and then repeated with a slight variation which adds to or reflects or contradicts the original meaning. For example, both the Bible and the Koran contain passages of highly poetic parallelism:

> *If you call them to the right path, they will not hear you. You find them looking towards you, but they cannot see you.*

> *But I, as a deaf man, heard not; and I was as a dumb man that openeth not his mouth.*
> *Thus I was a man that heareth not, and in whose mouth are no reproofs.*

The fifth pattern which Kaplan identifies is a common Oriental pattern. He calls this 'an approach by indirection'. The sentences circle round the topic, often defining something in terms of what it is not, and avoid any explicit judgement or conclusions.

Kaplan's analysis is interesting, even though you may not agree totally with his patterns and explanations. Certainly his suggestion of the importance of strict relevance in English writing is supported in the following case of a Thai postgraduate writing a thesis about population changes in northern Thailand. The first chapter of this thesis covered a general summary of the geography, history and culture of Thailand. The second chapter covered the same features, in more detail, of northern Thailand. In the third chapter, after fifty pages of this general introduction, the student began to provide information about population patterns. His Australian supervisor crossed out the whole first two chapters because they were 'not relevant' and suggested the student should have begun with his material in chapter three. His topic, the supervisor said, was the changing population in northern Thailand. Material to do with the geography, history and culture of Thailand, or even northern Thailand, would only be relevant if it explained significant points in the population pattern, and should only be introduced into the thesis when the data required explanation. Yet to the Thai student this direct 'English' approach seemed too blunt. It went against all his training in which a gradual approach to the central issues was preferred.

Although Kaplan was writing about differences in writing styles which arise from differences in national cultures, it is also true that each academic discipline is, to some extent, a 'sub-culture' in itself. Even in the 'international' languages of mathematics and science, there are significant differences within the branches of these disciplines, not just in the content of what is being studied but also in the acceptable ways of presenting that content in writing. For example, there are standard models for writing papers and reports in Chemistry and in Engineering, but they are different. And within each discipline there will be different criteria for deciding what is relevant; for example, what must be summarized in the Introduction and what can be included merely by a reference to previously published research. In both cases the stylistic aim will be brevity and clarity; but the way in which the material is presented, the use of statistics, of formulae, of graphic and illustrative material will vary, as a glance at journals in these two disciplines shows. In the Social Sciences and Humanities the differences between disciplines are even more marked.

So a student who is studying more than one discipline, maybe a first year student enrolled in courses in Zoology, Psychology, History and Sociology, must learn the styles acceptable to each of these four sub-cultures. The problem of coping with a range of disciplines is discussed in this comment by a Bangladesh undergraduate:

> I'd like to draw the reader's attention to one particular point: the reason for my fruitful progress can be mainly due to the fact I have devoted my three years of study to one particular subject, i.e. Biology. I would think that people who are doing, say, a combined Economics and Agriculture course, or Forestry and Computing, etc. would have to encounter much more problems than I have because then they'd have to be reading/writing in two dimensions throughout their study period, as I gather there are ways of writing a Computing assignment that are not particularly suitable in writing a Forestry field report.

If we return, therefore, to the first question asked at the beginning of this chapter — is it true that people from different cultures 'think differently'? — then the answer appears to be: 'Yes, in many cases they do'. And all students, even if they come from the same culture, must learn to 'think differently' in the different disciplines they choose to study. So it is essential for you to learn to be flexible in your style of thinking and writing so you can select the style which is most appropriate for each task you have to do.

In the next chapters we shall help you to prepare for the shifts in study behaviour you may have to make when you go abroad yourself. We shall begin by explaining the system of education and the ways in which students are expected to study in Australia. If you are planning to go to Britain, Canada or the United States, you will find supplementary information for these countries in the Appendices. In Chapter 5 we go on to examine in more detail the process of critical thinking which is expected of tertiary students in all these countries.

Summary

In this chapter we have looked at cultural variations in styles of thinking which may interfere with study in a foreign institution. We have also examined the influence of different cultures on the ways in which students learn and the styles they use for presenting their ideas. For many Asian students, successful study abroad involves the need to develop a more analytical and critical approach to learning.

MORE TO THINK ABOUT

1 For two of the subjects which you are presently studying, make a list of the things you have been required to do in the past week in each subject. Include activities which have taken place both inside the classroom and in your own study time. (If you are studying Chemistry, for example, your list might include such things as: writing up a description of an experiment, summarizing a section of your textbook, taking notes from the board or your teacher's dictation, memorizing atomic weights, calculating chemical equations, learning formulae for a test, lab work, and so on. Try to make your list as complete as possible.)

When you have finished this task, turn to Figure 1, Learning Styles, on p. 12. Next to each item on your list write:
   • the type of learning strategy, and
   • the learning approach
which best describes that item.

2 Talk to someone who has had experience of studying abroad. Ask this person about the problems he or she had in adjusting to different styles of learning in a foreign university or college. (You might start by asking this person to read the three student comments on pp. 13–14 and then discuss them.)

Find out about the **amount** of written and practical work that was required. What differences in **approach** to study did this person notice? If possible, get him or her to give you three Golden Rules for successful study abroad.

Discuss your findings with a fellow student, and compare each set of Golden Rules.

3 We have suggested in the last section of this chapter that there are important differences between disciplines of study, not only in content but also in the way that content is presented. As a way of judging this for yourself, take two textbooks (or journal articles) from different disciplines and examine the way in which the material in them is presented.

What differences can you notice in:
- the **physical organization** of the texts? (Are they broken up into sections? Do they use headings and sub-headings? Are there diagrams, illustrations, etc.?)
- the **intellectual organization** of the texts? (Are they mainly presenting facts and information (describing) or are they mainly discussing ideas (analysing)? Do they refer to other writers and researchers as the sources of their information and views? Do they present any conflicting or opposing views? Do they reach any conclusions?)
- the **styles of writing**? (Do different subjects have special 'languages' of their own?)

When you have identified some differences between the texts, discuss with your class possible reasons for these differences. Are they simply a matter of format, or are they related to differences between disciplines?

Undergraduate Studies

Chapter 3
Undergraduate Degree Courses

In explaining the structure of undergraduate degrees in this chapter, we are using the Australian university for our model. What we describe will apply in general terms to degree courses in other institutions and in other countries. There are, however, also some important differences. For more detailed information about Australian institutions, see the references listed at the end of this chapter. For variations that apply in Britain, Canada and the United States, consult Appendices 1–3.

Many Australian students when they first enter university or college feel as strange as if they were moving into a foreign country, an alien culture. They will already have completed twelve years of primary and secondary education. They will have been above-average pupils, successful enough to have gained admission to a tertiary institution on the basis of their state exams or school performance. Yet despite their past success they are often nervous. They are entering a very different world from their school surroundings.

The Australian academic year runs from March to November and is divided into either two semesters or three terms. The new students' first experience of the university is likely to be Orientation Week, an introductory week of activities for new students organized by senior students. During this week there is usually a preliminary talk or lecture in each first-year course, but it is mainly a time for student activities. There are many social events — films, parties, plays, dances; clubs and societies try to enrol new members; there are special tours of the libraries and talks on services available to students, such as medical services, student loans, and sport facilities. This is the week in which new students begin to get their bearings and become oriented to the university setting.

We shall describe in this chapter some features of the structure and workings of an Australian university which you will find helpful to know from the outset. (If you are intending to study at a college of advanced education or a technical institute there will be some variations on this structure. For specific information about individual tertiary institutions in Australia, consult the nearest Australian High Commission or Embassy.)

1 University titles

It is useful to know the official titles of university staff:

Chancellor	— formal head of the university but an honorary position usually held by a distinguished citizen.
Vice-Chancellor	— executive head of the university, nearly always an academic and holding the post for a five or seven year team.
Registrar *(or Academic Registrar)*	— senior administrator responsible for the routine management of the university, including admissions, fees, and exams.
Dean of Students	— a senior academic appointed to have special responsibility for student interests and welfare.

The university is divided into *Faculties* or *Schools*, such as the Faculty of Law, the Faculty of Economics, and the Faculty of Science. Each Faculty is composed of different *Departments*, such as the Department of Civil Engineering, the Department of Mining and Metallurgy and the Department of Surveying, all within the Faculty of Engineering.

Each Faculty has:

Dean	— head of the Faculty, usually a senior academic elected by the staff of all the Departments in the Faculty for a limited term, maybe two or three years.
Sub-deans	— elected academics who serve as advisers to students on the structure of their degree course and their academic progress.

Each Department has:

Head of Department	— usually a Professor but may be a

senior academic, responsible for the organization of the Department, including the teaching, staffing and research.

Professor — the most senior rank; there are seldom more than two Professors in any Department.

The other ranks in a Department are:

Reader
Senior Lecturer
Lecturer
Senior Tutor
Tutor

Outside the academic Departments, the university also appoints some staff to the post of:

Counsellor — adviser to students on matters of mental health and well-being, social welfare, and such areas as career and study skills advice.

2 Admission

Entry to universities in Australia is restricted.

At the undergraduate level there are three types of restriction which may apply:

General entry provisions: Each university sets a minimum score (aggregate of marks) which students must reach in their Year 12 or Higher School Certificate studies in order to gain entry. This minimum level is not very high in comparison with many overseas countries, e.g. at ANU in 1983 the top 50% of the local Year 12 school population qualified for general entry.

Quotas: General entry to a university does not necessarily guarantee entry to particular Faculties. Some highly popular Faculties, such as Law and Medicine, impose their own quotas. In such cases the number of students admitted is only a small percentage of those who apply. These are usually students with outstanding academic results at the Year 12 level.

Prerequisites: Certain Deparments also impose restrictions on entry based on the student's previous training in particular subjects or courses at the secondary level. For example, many Science courses require a pass in Chemistry at Year 12; Engineering students must have a certain level in Mathematics.

There is also a fourth kind of restriction — this one imposed by the student's own desire to study particular courses. Few universities offer the full range of academic courses. ANU, for example, has only five Faculties: Arts (Humanities and Social Sciences), Science (including Forestry), Law, Economics (including Commerce), and Asian Studies. If a student wished, therefore, to come to Australia to study Engineering or Agricultural Science, he could not do so at ANU but must go to one of the other universities or institutes.

The specific restrictions and the way in which they are applied vary, of course, with the individual universities, colleges and institutions. If you are seriously contemplating study abroad, you will need to consult the Embassy or High Commission of the country in which you wish to study, in order to obtain information about particular institutions and conditions of entry.

3 Undergraduate degree structure

New students must also learn how the degree course is structured. Students normally register in one Faculty and work towards a Bachelor's degree largely within that Faculty, finally gaining a Bachelor of Science (BSc), or a Bachelor of Economics (BEc), or a Bachelor of Engineering (BEng) degree. In some universities it is also possible to do a combined degree, such as an Economics/Science degree (BEcSc). Most pass degree courses require three years of full-time study, though some, such as Medicine or Law, take longer. If a student wants to gain an Honours degree, this requires an additional year of study after the pass degree has been completed at a high standard.

The structure of the degree course varies from one university to another and from one Faculty to another, but here is a fairly common pattern for a three-year pass degree in a Faculty of Economics (see diagram on page 25): There are three matters to notice about this course structure. Firstly, courses (also sometimes called units) may extend for either a full-year (consisting of three terms) or a half-year (semester). Secondly, in a three-year pass degree students are normally required to complete two majors (a *major* is a sequence of three units in one discipline — our student has completed majors in Economics and Accounting) and one sub-major (a *sub-major* is a sequence of two units in one discipline — our student has a sub-major in Political Studies). Thirdly, additional units to make up the number required for the degree — in this case 10 — will

First Year: four full-year units: (or equivalent)	Economics 1	Accounting 1	Politics 1	Statistics 1A & 1B (2 semester units)
Second Year: three full-year units: (or equivalent)	Economics 2	Accounting 2	Inter- national Politics	
Third Year: three full-year units: (or equivalent)	Economics 3	Accounting 3		Introduction to Computer Systems + Computing for Accounting (2 semester units)

normally be chosen according to the student's aims and interests. Our student, for example, chose to take two semester units in Computer Studies in her third year in order to improve her qualifications for the job market. The amount of choice a student has, however, varies with the degree being taken: in Medicine and Law, for example, it is common to find that all four first-year courses are compulsory. Where there is a choice, it is usually possible to change to another unit within the first few weeks of teaching if a student dislikes the one first selected.

By the time our student has completed the units set out in her plan, she will have satisfied the full requirements for a pass degree, a Bachelor of Economics. If she has gained high grades she could then continue for a fourth year and work for an Honours degree. In this final year she may have to enrol in certain courses on Economic Theory and Research Methods and she will also have to complete a sub-thesis, or a long essay, based on independent research. If she gains a good Honours degree, a 1st class or a 2A class Honours, then she would be eligible to proceed to postgraduate studies, for a Master's or a PhD degree.

4 Teaching system

Once a student is enrolled in a course, he must find out the lecture times and, once term has begun, sign up for a weekly tutorial meeting or, if he is studying Science, a weekly practical or laboratory session. Most courses, apart from foreign languages, have either two or three one-hour lectures each week. In some departments attendance at both lectures and tutorials is compulsory; in others it may be optional. The person giving the weekly lectures is referred to as the lecturer, even though he may hold the rank of reader or tutor.

Tutorials usually consist of small groups of students who meet with a staff member once a week for an hour to discuss topics related to the course. Again, the staff member leading the tutorial is referred to as the 'tutor' in this course even though he may hold a more senior rank; even professors may act as tutors in some courses. The ways in which tutorials operate vary a great deal and we shall look at this in more detail in Chapter 4.

In the Science departments practicals and laboratory sessions take the place of tutorials. These sessions usually last for two or three hours and are supervised by the lecturer and a number of assistants, called 'demonstrators', who are available to help students with their experiments and answer questions.

Students enrolled in Arts, Social Science, Law, and other non-Science degrees will also find that much of their learning takes place in the library. In most universities there is one central library and a number of smaller specialist libraries, maybe for Law or Science. The libraries are well-stocked with books and academic periodicals and are open for use by students until late every evening and during the weekends and vacation periods. Most books can be borrowed for private study at home but the books which are needed regularly by students in a large course may only be used in the library itself.

5 Assessment system

In some courses the students' performance is assessed wholly by a final formal exam; in others assessment is continuous, with each piece of written work and each short test counting towards the final grade; in many courses there is a mixture of continuous assessment and some form of final exam.

Exams can take a wide range of forms. Multiple-choice exams, in which students tick or circle their chosen answers, are not common in Australian universities. A combination of short-answer questions and some longer essay-type questions is more usual. Some exams are very formal and students cannot take any books or notes into the exam hall. Open-book exams, on the other hand, permit students to bring their textbooks, lecture notes or other materials into the exam room for use as references. Another common form of exam is the take-home exam, in which students are given the exam paper to take home for two or three days and write out their answers during this period. So there are many variations, depending on the policy of the Department in which the course is given.

In some courses students are given a numerical mark to indicate their level of performance; in some courses a letter grade is used; in others a Pass-Credit-Distinction is preferred. Here is a general explanation of the grading system:

level	letter grade	mark
Fail	N	below 50
Pass	P	50–64
Credit Hons 2B	C H2B	65–74
Distinction Hons 2A	D H2A	75–84
High Distinction Hons 1	HD H1	85–100

In some courses the two Distinction levels are referred to as Pass with Merit, and in others two levels of Pass are given: a P2 or Low Pass which does not allow students to proceed to the next level in the subject, and a P1 or High Pass which does.

So, all new students have a lot to learn about the strange environment of a university. You will not be the only student who finds the surroundings unfamiliar at first.

Summary

In this chapter we have summarized information which is useful for new undergraduates about the university system in Australia. (Supplementary information for Britain, Canada and the United States is given in the Appendices.) We have covered in some detail

- the titles of university staff,
- general admission procedures,
- the structure of the undergraduate degree,
- the teaching system within the university faculties, and
- some methods of assessment.

REFERENCES

Commonwealth Universities Yearbook, Association of Commonwealth Universities, London

Financial Aid for First Degree Study at Commonwealth Universities, Association of Commonwealth Universities, London

MORE TO THINK ABOUT

1 In the first two sections of this chapter we have discussed certain features of the structure of the university and of the undergraduate degree course in Australia. Compare this with the university system in your own country. In particular:

- make a list of the titles and functions of university staff which it would be useful for new students to know,
- construct a figure showing a typical undergraduate degree course in your own country (use the example on p. 25 as a model) and explain what regulations apply to it.

2 If it is possible to obtain a University or Faculty Handbook for an overseas university or college, study it and try to work out a degree course structure for yourself. (You may find some Handbooks in Embassies or your university library. Maybe a student who has returned from studying overseas will be able to lend you one.)

Discuss this with a fellow student or with students who have returned from study overseas and see whether your proposed course seems to meet all the official regulations.

3 Arrange a discussion in your class on the subject of Assessment. Questions you can cover would include:

- what is the purpose of assessment?
- what are the advantages and disadvantages of multiple-choice versus essay exams?
- what benefits and problems can you see arising with the open-book and take-home styles of exam we have described in this chapter?

(If you want to practise a more formal tutorial discussion, ask three members of your group to make a short (5 minute) presentation, each speaker discussing one of the aspects listed above. Then the whole class can join in with questions and discussion.)

Chapter 4
What Academics Expect of Undergraduates

In this chapter we shall look first at the school background of Australian university students, which should give you some idea of the ways in which these students are prepared for tertiary study. Academic staff assume

- that all their students have been through a reasonably common training in how to learn,
- that they have the necessary background for the subjects they choose to study, and
- that they are able to express their ideas well in writing and speech.

You may find it useful to compare the ways in which these students are encouraged to study with your own school experience.

We then move on to the particular demands which university study makes of all students, whether Australian or from overseas. The final section of this chapter covers the further developments in styles of thinking and learning necessary for students continuing to an Honours degree, and possibly from there to postgraduate studies.

Secondary school background

Australian students entering university have completed six years of secondary schooling. The schools they come from vary from public (government) day schools to private day or boarding schools, often established by different branches of the Christian church. Some schools follow a fairly rigid syllabus leading to a state-wide examination; others develop their own syllabuses and, in place of an external examination, assessment is conducted by the teachers themselves.

Most schools are well-equipped with libraries, science and language laboratories, and sporting facilities. The teachers are qualified specialists and are well paid. They are either trained in a three-year course at a teacher training college or they are university graduates who have taken an additional one year teaching qualification course.

On a national average about 35% of pupils continue to the two final years of secondary school, even though school attendance is only compulsory between the ages of six and fifteen years. In these two years students begin to specialize in their course of studies. Some may choose to follow a Science stream; others may choose Arts (Humanities), Commerce or Technical Arts as their main area of concentration.

At the same time as they are beginning to specialize in their subject areas, students are encouraged to become more independent learners. How is this done? Let us look into some Year 12 classrooms in a modern school. What are we likely to find?

The first room we come to is full of noise and activity; most of the students are huddled in threes and fours around workbenches, talking and occasionally calling out in excitement. One boy leaves his group, goes across to the glass cabinet on the wall and takes an instrument from it; a girl drifts over to another group of her friends in order to watch their progress. Moving closer we can see that they are dissecting rats; it is a biology lesson. In a quieter corner at the back of the room three students, sitting separately, are writing up accounts of the experiment which they have just finished. As we leave, there is a burst of laughter from one group and, looking back, we see the teacher for the first time; she is joining in the laughter and pointing out to one of the students his mistake in confusing the rat's heart with its liver.

The next room is much calmer, although it seems to be a student who is conducting the lesson. He is standing at the front reading a poem to a group of about twenty others, including the teacher, who sit in a semi-circle around him. He stops reading and asks them for an opinion about the poem. There is an embarrassed silence for a moment; people look at the floor and the ceiling, shuffle their feet, too shy or uncertain to speak first. Then one girl quietly says that she liked the poem; it has a mood of joy and freedom. Silence again. Another girl points out an image she didn't understand; she thinks it's too difficult, too obscure. The boy next to her disagrees. Others join in; suddenly there is a babble of talk, and the class has become a cluster of separate conversations. The boy at the front looks confused. He tries to speak over the noise but cannot make himself heard. The noise goes on until the teacher claps her hands for silence. As we go out the door we hear her talking to the boy: 'Edward, you read the poem well and you were beginning to get a discussion going. But you must try to guide the speakers more. Direct who is to speak first . . .'

In the library nearby a group of six students is working very quietly together, writing up the results of a series of surveys they have been doing over the past month. A new major road is planned for the suburb in which the school is located, and these students have been trying to determine where the road should go. They have made up a questionnaire and distributed it to residents in the area; they have interviewed shopkeepers and factory owners; last week they spoke to members of the local Council and town engineers to find out the official views. Out of all this information they have planned what they think is the best route for the new road, and now they are writing a report of their findings. Each student is responsible for a different section of the report which they will present, orally, in two days to their classmates and then send a copy on to the Council itself.

Of course not all schools and teachers are as flexible as this. Some follow a more rigid syllabus and a more traditional teaching style. In such schools the teacher does most of the talking and writing on the blackboard. He demonstrates a lab experiment and the students follow him, step by step. There is often one course textbook which covers nearly all that the students are required to know for that subject. The emphasis here is on learning factual information accurately, and teaching is directed towards a final examination. This kind of teaching is more common in science and technical subjects than in social sciences or humanities. Yet even in such classes some independent study is expected, and students are not encouraged to sit passively during lessons. They must volunteer to answer questions and join in discussions; they must make their own notes and write regular assignments.

In all schools, however, there is emphasis on written work both in assignments during the term and in exams. The assignments normally ask students to **describe** some situation or phenomenon, for example:

Describe the reproductive system of the kangaroo.

Summarize the main climatic features of the monsoon areas of Southeast Asia.

or to **explain** something, either directly or through comparison, for example:

Explain the causes of the American War of Independence.

Compare the policy of free trade with the policy of tariff protection in the Pacific basin.

Sometimes these topics have already been covered in class by the teacher; sometimes the student must look up the information independently in the textbook or by using other books in the school library. The amount of information required is limited and the student's task is to select and summarize it clearly. Though class discussions often involve argument and different points of view, written assignments usually focus on topics which are less controversial.

Most exams require written answers, either brief paragraphs or full-length essays (say, 500 words). Multiple-choice tests are used only for certain subjects, such as Chemistry or Biology, where factual recall is important, or in very limited ways, such as one segment of a final test. It is important, therefore, for these students to be able to interpret questions and express their ideas quickly, fluently and in correct English.

So it is this background that secondary school students bring to their tertiary studies.

First year at university

Approximately 17% of Australian secondary school students continue to either universities or colleges for tertiary studies. Now they have to meet very different demands. Tertiary students are expected to act and work more independently:

- in making decisions about their courses, their study and use of time,
- in making use of the resources and facilities of the institution, and
- in developing their own ideas and capacity to make judgements.

The change is probably more obvious in Humanities courses than in Science, and at university than at college, but all tertiary study requires greater self-reliance.

Let us look more closely at some of these changes which you, as a first year student, will probably have to make.

1 General independence and self-reliance

New students can find the apparent freedom of tertiary study a bit bewildering. Listen to these first-year students talking about some of the problems they had while settling in to university life.

> Chris (a Humanities student): I couldn't believe it when I first got here — only twelve hours of classes a week (at school I had almost twice that). Twelve hours — and that's total. The rest of the week was mine, I could do what I wanted. It was suddenly like being let out

of gaol. Even the twelve hours I had, I didn't **have** to attend, you know, it wasn't compulsory except for three of the tutorials. You decide for yourself if you want to go, if you think it's worth it. Well, I didn't go a lot in first term — and suddenly bang, it's the end of term, I've got three essays due and a test. And my tutor picks this time to tell me that I'm supposed to be doing two hours in the library for every hour in class.

Anna (a Science student): It wasn't so much the timetable that surprised me. In fact if you count all the lab sessions as well as lectures, I've got more classes now than at school. Twenty-three hours. It's the fact that you're on your own. I mean I know the teachers are still there and the demonstrators will help you in a prac. if you're stuck on a problem, or show you how to do an experiment. But if you don't do the work, that's your decision. They leave you to plan all your own work. At school, if you didn't hand your Chem. prac. books in each week for correction, the teacher would come round and ask you why. And keep at you till you did it. Here it's not the teacher's problem if you don't do work or get good marks — it's yours.

This new way of life brings freedom, therefore, but it can create other pressures.

David (an Economics student from Hong Kong, who completed his last two years of high school in Australia): I live in a Hall where I do all my own cooking. It's much cheaper than the residences where they provide meals, but I have to allow time to buy food and for cooking and cleaning. Also, I can cook proper Chinese food and not eat Australian food which is all right for some but not my stomach. So it takes time, but I prefer it.

But perhaps the biggest problem of all comes from the sheer size of modern urban universities. Helen, a country girl beginning a degree in Social Science, reflects this view:

Uni. is just so big. So impersonal. One of my classes — Political Science — has three hundred students in it. That's incredible. At school, the biggest class I was ever in was thirty. Here the lecturers don't even know your name — how can they? You pass in the corridor and you think 'Hey, Dr Barrington, I'm in your class. Hey, don't you notice me?' and they just look right through you as though they've never seen you before . . . total strangers.

There will be other staff of course, such as tutors who lead small groups, who do know your name and who are helpful to individuals, especially new students. But Helen is right; academics are often remote.

The informal and apparently casual nature of some university teaching can be confusing at first. Lectures may not be compulsory. In many Science departments tutorials may be optional. In some courses the assignments and short tests during the term are optional. And each week there are public lectures and seminars being held at the university which you can attend if you wish. After the much stricter organization of secondary school, you may find it difficult to decide for yourself how much use you will make of these informal resources. Your decisions will rest on your interest in a subject and the amount of time you can usefully devote to deepening this interest. An apparently informal discussion or question period in a lecture or tutorial can often give you valuable clues into current controversies or problems.

You must decide for yourself whether or not you make use of these informal resources for learning. Developing motivation and effective study habits is now your responsibility.

2 *Effective use of learning resources*

Few academic staff are trained teachers. They are appointed for their expertise in research, which may be very specialized — not merely, for instance, in Zoology but in the reproductive system of marsupial rats, not merely in Economics but in international trade balances in the Pacific basin. They are employed to teach undergraduates and graduates, but they are also expected to continue with their research and, for the majority of university lecturers, these research interests come before their interest in teaching. So, as a student, you will need to be capable of learning almost independently of 'teachers'. This means making effective use of all the learning resources within the institution.

These resources include:

a *lectures*: Lecture classes may be very large, as many as 400 students, and the lecturer usually presents his material very formally. There is seldom any opportunity for discussion or asking questions; you are expected just to listen and take notes. Some lecturers provide outline notes for each lecture they give, and in a few courses the lectures may follow closely your course textbook. Generally, however, these aids are not available and your own notes provide the only record of the lecture content.

What material is covered in lectures? Most commonly the lectures provide the basic content and ideas you need to know. They cover the important case studies and examples which should interest you. They introduce you to the work of experts in your field of study. They provide a common base from which you can work on more specialized topics in tutorials, essays and research projects. Attendance at lectures is seldom compulsory, but poor attendance may lead to problems later on when you have to prepare for tests or exams which are usually based on the lecture material.

b *tutorials and laboratory sessions*: Tutorial groups are small, usually between 10 and 15 students. In these weekly meetings with the same tutor you get a chance to break through the impersonality of the lecture course; you can become known to your tutor and you can make friends with other students in the group.

What happens in tutorials? This varies a good deal with individual tutors. In some tutorials you may find yourself discussing material already covered in the lectures, which gives you the chance to raise questions about any points not clear to you. In other tutorials each student in the group in turn has to lead the discussion on a particular topic which supplements the material being covered in the lectures. Other tutorials may provide practice in applying operations or techniques described in the lectures — this is common in maths, statistics and computer courses. A common aim for all tutorials is to give you practice in expressing your ideas orally and in discussing, criticizing and arguing about points raised by the tutor and other students.

Tutorials, therefore, make more demands than lectures: you are expected to be prepared to join in the discussion and be ready to express an opinion — and defend it. Most new students at first feel shy about presenting their ideas publicly, about criticizing the ideas of others and risking criticism of their own. Yet, once they become accustomed to this form of open discussion, students commonly report that a good tutorial is the most interesting and valuable part of a course.

In Science courses the compulsory lab sessions, often called 'pracs' (practicals), are an important part of your scientific training. It is here that you gain the experimental and manual skills which you will need for later scientific work. In these labs you develop competence in using equipment and working by yourself or in a small team. To help you there are lab technicians who assist with apparatus and materials, and demonstrators who supervise your experiments and can offer advice and answer questions. Prac sessions are usually tightly organized to supplement the content of the lectures and all students are expected to complete all of the experiments and tasks prescribed for each week of the semester. In some courses you may also go on field trips.

c *libraries*: In all courses, but particularly if you are studying Humanities, Social Sciences or Law, you are expected to make use of the library for your own reading and research. This means you must learn how to use the catalogues, the indexes to periodicals, the audio-visual materials (including taped lectures and other recorded programmes), the language laboratories and other research tools. If you are in a large first year course, many of the books you need most frequently may be on a special Short Loan system which means you can only borrow them for a restricted period — maybe two hours — and you can only read them in the library itself. First-year Science and Technology students usually have less need to use the library at this early stage of their studies; more time and emphasis are placed on lab sessions.

Most people feel bewildered when they first encounter a complex library system. However, there are special staff (Readers' Advisers) whose job it is to help students understand how the library works. They frequently run courses in library use early in the academic year and they are available to help you with any problems you have in locating books or tracking down information.

d *students and staff*: As we noticed earlier, the general atmosphere of a university is impersonal. At first you may feel too overawed by your lecturers to venture into their offices and 'trouble' them with your questions about a lecture or an essay or a problem sheet. Yet most academic staff, from professors to tutors, are quite willing to talk with students about matters relating to their work in the course. But they will expect you to take the first step by coming to talk with them.

Your fellow students can also be a useful source of information and help. Some students are hesitant to seek help from others in case this is seen as 'cheating' or taking advantage of their friends. However, tertiary study is often best managed co-operatively. A study group of three or four students discussing issues raised in a lecture, or working out the problem in a weekly assignment, or revising for an exam can be a very effective way of learning. Particularly if you are living in a residence you should find it easy to form such a group.

Finally, most Australian universities and colleges employ counsellors, study advisers, and English language tutors who can assist you with your studies. These services are usually free and available to all enrolled students. Nearly all students, at some point in their career, make use of them.

3 Development of critical thinking and effective presentation of ideas

So far we have discussed the changes needed in the way you organize your study and we have described the different resources that become available to you as you move from school to university. The most important change, however, is not a matter of study strategies or resources but a matter of **styles of thinking**. In fact we regard the development of an analytical and critical style of thinking as so vital, so close to the heart of university studies, that we will take the whole of Chapter 5 to explain this process in detail. The brief comments we make here, therefore, are simply intended to introduce this change to you. We shall start with an example.

Imagine a Year 12 student at a secondary school who has been asked to write a 600-word History essay on the topic:

What were the causes of the Second World War, 1939–1945?

In order to answer this question satisfactorily, the student would be expected to read the one or two chapters from her textbook in modern history that deal with this subject. She would make notes, listing the causes set out in these chapters, and then write the essay by combining her notes in a clear sequence. The only judgement she might need to make would be to decide whether to start with the most important cause and work through to the least important, or whether to start at the other end and work up to the major cause.

Now imagine a first-year university student who has also been set an essay on the causes of the Second World War. How would his task differ from that of the secondary school student?

For a start, the topic would probably be worded differently, making it both more precise and more complex.

To what extent was the outbreak of war in 1939 caused by the rise of German nationalism?

The essay would be much longer, perhaps 1500 or 2000 words, and therefore the extent of research and depth of detail required would be much greater. But, most importantly, the student would not be able to base his answer on information gathered from just one or two textbooks; he would be expected to read much more widely and critically. Reading 'widely' might mean reading and taking notes from eight or nine texts or articles. While doing this, the student becomes aware that there is not one 'correct' answer to the question, but at least eight or nine possible answers. Every historian he consults has a different view or interpretation of the importance of the rise of German nationalism in relation to the outbreak of World War II. Therefore he must read 'critically', that is with a questioning mind rather than as a sponge simply soaking up all information on the page. Critical reading means trying to identify where the writers differ and why; it means trying to evaluate the strengths and weaknesses of each writer's argument. Finally it means coming to an independent **judgement** of the whole question: how important was the rise of German nationalism in causing the Second World War, and what other factors must also be considered as significant causes of the war?

Let us suppose that our student has read widely and critically, and that he has come to an independent judgement about the whole question. Is that all his lecturer would expect of him? No; he must now **persuade** the lecturer that his judgement is acceptable. That is, he must assemble his ideas, facts and other evidence and write them out in such a way that they convince the reader. He must **argue** the case that German nationalism was — or was not — a major cause of the war, showing at each step of his argument the reasons why he thinks that way. And he must do so in clear correct English, set out in the particular essay format required by the Department.

We can summarize what is expected in a university essay by listing the four main criteria which, together with factual accuracy, most academic staff in our own university use to assess an essay:

1 It is expected that the essay will be *clearly focused on the set topic and will deal fully with its central concerns.*
2 It is expected that the essay will be *the result of wide and critical reading.*
3 It is expected that the essay will present *a reasoned argument.*
4 It is expected that the essay will be *competently presented.*

Only the final criterion, competent presentation, deals with aspects of style, grammar, and format. The other three criteria focus on qualities of critical thinking and independent judgement.

Some of the criteria for writing essays apply also to lab reports. The material in the report must be relevant to its aim, the report should be correctly and well expressed, and so on. But there are differences as well. The most obvious of these relates to the structure and lay-out of the report. Though there will be variations among departments, the standard format includes the following sections: Introduction (including Aim), Materials and Methods, Results, and Discussion. Within each section there are further 'rules', or conventions, governing such things as the use of sub-headings, tables, diagrams, illustrations, etc. The Results section, you will be told, must

include all the results of your experiments and must have only results in it. Any interpretation of these results or attempts to relate
them to the previous research you mentioned in your Introduction
must be saved for the Discussion section. As well as these differences in structure between the essay and the lab report, there are
also differences in style. A key criterion for scientific style, for example, is brevity. Brevity is less important in the essay, in which you
are encouraged to express ideas in an elaborate form. In a lab report you come closest to this more extended style of writing within
the Discussion section. Here you are encouraged to question and to
criticize. (Why did I get these results? How can I account for the
differences between my results and those predicted by the theory?
Are there weaknesses in the experimental design and methods?
etc.)

First-year students are often worried at being asked to criticize or
evaluate the ideas and theories they read in books or learn in lectures. 'I am only a student. How can I know whether this is better
than that? How can I disagree with my lecturer? How can I question
the authority of a textbook?' Yet developing the capacity to make
valid judgements is a major objective of higher education. If a student writes an essay based merely on the notes he has taken in lectures or on the summary of the material in one book, the lecturer is
likely to criticize him sharply: 'All this comes from my lecture. I
know this already. Use your brain, not mine,' or 'This essay merely
repeats Smith's article. I can read Smith more easily in print. What
else have you read? What do **you** think?'

4 Academic disciplines as sub-cultures: the need to adapt

The criteria for essays which we listed above are fairly common
across all disciplines. But there are also important differences in the
way each discipline directs your thinking.

Let us take one item of content — an Australian Aboriginal folktale — and show how it would be used in different disciplines. In an
Anthropology course the folktale might be used in comparison with
tales from other tribal groups to show the relationship between social organization and folktale motifs. In Linguistics the same tale
might become an object for grammatical study; or a text for practising translation. In an Australian History course it would be used as
a source for pre-European history; in a Law course it might even be
the basis for a discussion of Aboriginal land rights. In Literature the
tale would be taken as an example of a particular literary genre; in
Comparative Religion or Philosophy it might be used to illustrate

certain spiritual traditions. Thus, although in each case the content is the same, each discipline analyses and uses the folktale in different ways and for different purposes.

University students, as we saw in Chapter 3, normally study four subjects in separate disciplines (four courses in different departments) in their first year. You can see, therefore, that one of the adaptations required for successful study is learning to recognize the special interests of **each** of your disciplines. That takes time, just as it takes time to learn the special 'language', particularly the vocabulary, which each discipline uses. What you are doing is learning the 'culture' of each discipline.

Understanding and handling the differences underlying academic disciplines is hard for all new students. At our university, for example, we have tried to identify the special problems first-year students have in bridging the gap between secondary and tertiary studies. Here are some of the main problems from our list.

Many first-year students have difficulty in:
- distinguishing between disciplines, i.e. recognizing that each discipline has its own method of analysis;
- learning to use competently the highly specialized languages of these methods of analysis;
- adjusting to unfamiliar disciplines;
- learning to think critically and analytically.

Clearly you should not expect to make all of the adjustments we have been describing at the same pace or with the same degree of success. You may find it easier, because of previous training or for some other reason, to adjust to the sub-culture of Accounting than, say, that of Economics. In our own work we frequently see students who are receiving very high grades for essays and tests in two of their courses and quite low marks in the others — yet they claim they are putting equal time and energy into each. By the end of first year much of this unevenness disappears as students gradually adjust to all four disciplines. But some differences can persist, or become even more pronounced. You may find, for example, that, despite your best efforts, you simply cannot do or do not want to make the necessary adjustments to succeed in Economics; if so, this is a discipline you might decide to drop in your later years of study.

Later undergraduate years and Honours year studies

After your first year, courses become more specialized and classes are smaller. Now you are expected to work more independently of your lecturers. For example, you are no longer given a list of suggested readings for an essay; now you must find your own sources in the library. You may be expected to develop your own research topics or design your own experiments. Assignments will be longer — 3000- or 5000-word essays instead of the first-year 1500-word length — and will deal more specifically with theories and concepts. In Science courses written assignments will no longer consist of lab reports and occasional short descriptive or summarizing essays; now you must apply theories, analyse, and evaluate. If you take Humanities courses, much of your time continues to be spent in reading, in writing essays and in presenting tutorial papers. Both the quantity and quality of your work, however, is expected to increase. And much of the increased load comes in the area of independent study. The number of hours you spend in formal lectures, labs and tutorials is usually fewer than in first-year.

If you gain a good final grade in a first-year course — usually at least a Credit — you may then be eligible to work for an Honours degree rather than a Pass degree. This normally means that you work at Honours level in **one** of your major subjects. The procedure for working towards an Honours degree varies greatly among universities and between departments. In some cases an Honours student must take particular courses within the Department, usually courses requiring theoretical studies, and must pass them at a high level. In some cases Honours students are grouped in separate tutorials and must complete extra assignments. In most cases Honours students take an additional year to complete their degree and, during the final Honours year, they must write a sub-thesis which requires some independent research.

The advantage of graduating with an Honours degree is that it enables you, if you have gained either a First Class or Upper Second Honours, to continue to postgraduate studies. (There are other routes to postgraduate degrees in some universities, but an Honours undergraduate degree is both the most common and the preferred training.) Only a few selected students complete an Honours programme; for example at our university there may be 350 students in the first-year Political Science course and only ten students will continue to complete their fourth-year Honours course. Of those ten Honours students, probably only four will continue to a Master's degree and maybe two of these will finally enrol for the PhD degree. But the Honours sub-thesis is the first formal step towards independent academic research.

Conclusion

In this chapter we have outlined for you the main features of the secondary school and undergraduate education of a typical student in Australia. We have not made direct comparisons with education systems in Asia or other parts of the world. For one thing, there are too many variations for such comparisons to be useful. Besides, you yourself know far better than anyone else how your own experience can be compared with the Australian system as we have explained it.

The one aspect we have stressed in all this explanation is the necessity for adjustment. Each level of education and each discipline makes different demands. The adjustments you must make are both cultural and intellectual. You are not merely required to learn new and different material; you must also master new ways of thinking and studying. This is a problem for Australian students in Australian universities; it is a problem for students in your own country in your own universities; it is a particular problem for overseas students studying in a foreign institution. For such students the problem is closely related to competence in language, but it is more complex than mere fluency in English. And in the next chapter we shall examine in more detail the nature of this complexity as it arises in the need to think critically and analytically.

Summary

We have looked at the styles of teaching and learning used in secondary school — the background training common to most undergraduates.

The central section of this chapter covers the changes which are necessary when a student moves to undergraduate studies. These include:
- emphasis on independence and self-reliance in studying,
- the need to make efficient use of learning resources, such as lectures, tutorials and labs, libraries, and staff,
- development of critical thinking and the ability to present ideas effectively, and
- the need to adapt to the differing demands of different disciplines.

The further development of these skills and attitudes in the later years of the Pass or Honours degree is also summarized.

MORE TO THINK ABOUT

1 In one section of this chapter we discussed some of the adjustments students must make in their first year of university study.

Using the same headings as we have used:
- general independence and self-reliance
- effective use of learning resources (lectures, tutorials and lab sessions, libraries, students and staff)
- development of critical thinking and effective presentation of ideas,

make notes for each of these areas pointing out the similarities and differences between what we have described and your **present** methods of learning.

2 One point we have emphasized in this chapter is the need to develop your own motivation for study. What are the main motivations for your current course of study at school or university? List seven factors which are influential, e.g. family, career, interest in subject, etc.

Compare your seven items with the list made by a fellow student. Discuss to what extent each motive is externally imposed (i.e. other people's motives for you) and which are internal (i.e. your own ambitions).

3 Interview one of your fellow students about his or her experience as a secondary school student. Ask and make notes about:
- the syllabus (who sets it? what forms of assessment are used? etc.)
- the resources of the school (is there a library? what laboratory facilities? etc.)
- the teachers (what qualifications are they required to have? what is their standing in society? etc.)
- the teaching style (how formal/informal? is the teacher seen as the only learning resource? is independent work encouraged? is questioning encouraged? etc.)

Compare your notes with those made by other members of your class and discuss the extent to which your secondary education has prepared you to meet the kinds of academic expectations we have described in this chapter.

Chapter 5
Critical Thinking

We have talked a lot so far about the importance of critical thinking in tertiary study. We have said that you need to use this style of thinking in listening to lectures, in reading for essays and tutorials, in participating in tutorial discussions and, most obviously, in developing a 'reasoned argument' in your essays and reports. It is time now to examine more closely what we mean by this term. We shall do this mostly in a practical way — by looking at some actual examples of tasks that students face in their first year of study at an Australian university. But first, what can be said in a more general way about critical thinking and the related act of analysis?

In broad terms, being critical means making careful or exact **judgements**. The critical thinker, therefore, is someone who approaches his material with the ultimate intention of judging its worth or value. He arrives at this point of judgement through a process of systematic **analysis** and **questioning**.

1 Analysis

What do we mean by analysis? Think of a chemist analysing an unknown substance. She tries to identify it and say what its properties are by reducing it to its simple elements. She breaks it down. She is then in a position to perceive the relationships between the separate elements. In the same way a researcher who is studying a complex topic — like the causes of a war, or the origins of a religious system, or the evolutionary effects of isolation on some species — will try to distinguish the different elements so that he can then study each of them separately, and their relationships. Thus he will try to decide:

- what each element is,
- what evidence there is for its existence or nature,
- how it relates to other elements, and
- how important it is.

2 Critical analysis

In the process of conducting his analysis, the researcher asks himself questions about the material he is studying. There are two types or levels of question which he may ask. The first consists of questions which are designed to clarify the facts. The chemist, for example, in trying to identify a substance, poses questions about its physical properties (what is the colour of the substance? its atomic weight? its reaction to other substances? etc). An historian, in trying to identify the causes of a war, is also interested in facts (what was the order of events in time? what are the sources of evidence for this sequence of events? etc).

The second type of question is not concerned with clarifying facts but with making judgements — judgements about the worth or value or truth of the subject being studied. For the historian the question is no longer simply: what are the sources of evidence for a sequence of events but **how valid** are those sources? are the documents being used first-hand accounts, or second-hand reports? are they supported by other sources? is there suspicion of bias or inaccuracy? Similarly the chemist, in trying to establish certain facts about the substance she is investigating, will ask herself questions about the value of her analysis: are the instruments of measurement the most appropriate and exact? are the experimental procedures being used exhaustive? is there more than one way of explaining the facts established in the analysis?

When they begin in this way to ask questions and make judgements about the value of the material being analysed, the researchers are moving over into the area of **critical analysis**. Notice that the words 'critical' and 'criticism' are not being used here in the purely negative sense in which they are often used in ordinary speech, not just to point out weaknesses. Rather they mean an attempt to judge the good as well as the bad; to distinguish the valid from the invalid, strengths from weaknesses. Notice too that the actual questions which are asked vary with the discipline: the questions appropriate to Chemistry might be quite inappropriate in History, and the other way around.

3 The context of critical analysis

A critical approach to knowledge and ideas is desirable in all areas of university study — in lectures, in seminar discussions, in independent reading. But in the context of essay and assignment writing, such an approach becomes essential. This emphasis on criticism may be less important in the first years of study in science and technology than it is in humanities and social sciences. Lab reports, for example, are usually more concerned with problem-solving, with learning new techniques and with demonstrating basic principles than with developing arguments about conflicting ideas or evidence. In later years of study, however, when there is a greater emphasis on theory, students are encouraged to be critical. They are expected to read widely and to write extended essays and assignments rather than short factual reports. In writing of this kind, a critical approach becomes essential. (An example of what this means in a scientific context is dealt with later.)

Let us look now at what a critical approach to knowledge requires in practice. Consider these two first-year essay topics:

Examine the theories of human nature held by Lao-tzu, Mencius, Hsun-tzu and Wang Ch'ung. To what extent are they conflicting? (History)

'Furthermore I am convinced that Natural Selection has been the most important, but not the exclusive means of modification.' Discuss this statement by Charles Darwin, using appropriate examples or experimental evidence to develop your argument. (Zoology)

In the first topic the phrase 'To what extent . . .' makes clear that students are being required to make a **judgement** about the degree of similarity and difference between the theories mentioned. In the second topic there are two indications of a similar requirement: first, the word 'Discuss . . .' (which demands an **analysis** of what can be said both for and against Darwin's statement) and second, the phrase '. . . your argument' (which demands a reasoned **judgement** of Darwin's claim in the light of scientific evidence).

In many topics the requirement for a critical approach is not explicitly stated, for example:

Compare and contrast theories of learned versus innate aggression. (Psychology)

Analyse the causes and effects of a shift in the savings-income schedule. (Economics)

Nevertheless in both of these topics a critical approach is required. The tasks specified in the first topic — **comparison** and **contrast** — are never final objectives but are always carried out for some larger purpose. The student must always ask himself: 'Why am I comparing these? What is the purpose of the contrast?' In this case the purpose is to reach a judgement about which set of theories is more correct, more convincing, has more reliable evidence to support it. Similarly the task of **analysing** something which is required by the second topic always provokes the questions: 'Analyse for what purpose? To what end?' In this case the purpose is to reach a judgement about how particular causes bring about particular effects, and about which causes and effects are more important than others. The word 'critically' is so fundamentally assumed by lecturers who set essay topics that they often neglect to say it explicitly.

Critical thinking, therefore, involves:

systematic **analysis**

— based on a **questioning** attitude to the material being analysed and the methods being used, and

— governed by the overall purpose of reaching a **judgement**.

Let us see what this means in practice.

a *analysing an essay topic*

A first year class in Psychology was set the task of writing an essay of 2000 words on the following topic:

> *Intelligence testing today is a very sensitive issue. Analyse the factors (biological, environmental and measurement) that are the primary sources of variation in IQ scores.*

The students were given a reading list of 6–8 papers and books. They were told that if they felt they needed further information, they could find sources for it by looking through the list of references and suggested readings at the end of each of the recommended texts.

In reading this topic, the first thing you may have noticed is that there appear to be three different factors influencing IQ scores: biology, environment and measurement. The students' task was to 'analyse' these factors. What does this involve? Here is an outline of the process of analysis, following the steps we discussed at the start of this chapter.

Topic: *Intelligence testing today is a very sensitive issue. Analyse the factors (biological, environmental and measurement) that are the primary sources of variation in IQ scores.*

1st Step **Analysis**	*deciding what each factor is*:
	e.g. biology: genetically inherited traits, capacities...
	environment: class, culture, family background...
	measurement: the way in which actual IQ testing is carried out...

Adopting a questioning and critical attitude	e.g. What is IQ anyway? What is the biological basis of IQ? Where does it reside and how do we know? Can we ever define all of the environmental factors?
2nd Step **Analysis**	*establishing what evidence there is for each factor*: e.g. experiments conducted on twin children reared in different environments in order to distinguish between the influences of biology and environment ...
Questioning and criticism	e.g. Are these experiments valid? Did the experimenters use a big enough sample to get reliable results? How can we be sure that the environments were in fact different? Or that, even though the experimental subjects were twins, their biological inheritance was identical?
3rd Step **Analysis**	*clarifying the relationships between the factors*: e.g. the connection, if any, between an environmental factor like class and the way in which IQ is measured ...
Questioning and criticism	e.g. Are IQ tests class/culture free? Or do they always reflect the cultural background of the testers? Do the tests assume a certain level of schooling? Or a certain level of competence in the standard language?
4th Step **Analysis**	*reaching some conclusion about the factors*: e.g. ranking in terms of importance ... concluding that no ranking is possible, given the current controversy about the quality of the evidence ...
Questioning and criticism	e.g. If the three factors are not entirely separable, can we ever say that one factor is dominant? Is there a strong political and cultural element in the interpretation of data? Are we even sure these three are the primary factors? Are there other factors just as important as these three?

Notice that the first step in adopting a critical attitude seems to be a matter of asking questions, particularly questions of:

Definition — What exactly is this thing (idea, fact, argument, theory) we are discussing?

Comparison and Contrast — How is it like or different from other related things?

Judgement — How good is the evidence for it?
Are there alternative ways of viewing it?
What is its overall importance?

b *summary and argument*

Let us look now at another essay topic, taking this process of analysis and criticism one step further. A first-year class in Anthropology was set the task of writing an essay of 1500 words on the following topic:

Describe the potlatch and discuss the more recent views of its functions.

Once again the students were provided with an initial reading list of 6–7 books and papers and told they could trace further materials for themselves.

The first part of the task — '*Describe the potlatch ...*' — proved relatively straightforward, a matter of recorded fact. (A potlatch, they soon learnt, was a gift-giving ceremony common amongst the Indian tribes of the north-west coast of North America.) The second part — '*... discuss the more recent views of its functions*' — proved much more difficult. There were some initial matters of definition to be tackled: what time span is implied by 'more recent'? (50 years? 100? Since the Second World War? Since some decisive moment in the history of Anthropology? Since a particular document was published about this ceremony?) This question could only be answered, the students rightly decided, by asking the lecturer what his intention was. Another matter of definition concerned the word 'functions'. What is meant by the 'function' of a ceremony? This question could only be answered by reference to the way in which anthropologists use the word, which might be quite different from the way in which it is used in other disciplines, for example in Biology or Psychology.

The students' next task was to go to the readings to discover what views anthropologists had about the functions of the potlatch. (The fact that the plural 'views' is used in the topic suggests immediately that there is more than one possible interpretation.)

Look now at the extract on pages 50–52 from one student's essay

What is happening in the text?

Which key words help us to understand what is happening in the text?

THE TEXT

General introduction, including a definition of the key term 'function'

Recent views of the function of the potlatch, that is, the contribution the institution made to the society, differ considerably. One function attributed to the potlatch of the Kwakiutl tribe is that of ensuring population survival. Stuart Piddocke (1950, p. 283–287) proposes that, prior to access to European markets, the Indians often faced food shortages and, although the area was comparatively rich in food resources, local and seasonal variations in food supply meant that 'scarcity of food was an ever-present threat' for the individual *numayms* or kinship groups (1950, p. 287).

Student's summary (with quotations) of view A

Performance of the potlatch, motivated by the desire for prestige, effected a redistribution of resources and ensured that those groups experiencing temporary hardship would survive. Therefore, according to Piddocke (1950, p. 298), the potlatch system enabled a larger population to live in the area than otherwise could have occurred.

Introduction of a comparison with view A leading to

Suttles, in a more recent publication, has an almost identical view of the function performed by the potlatch in the coastal Salish tribe (Suttles, 1960 a, p. 296–305). He believes that the distribution of food at potlatches between *numayms* relieved shortages and also tended to redistribute the wealth of a *numaym* with more consistently plentiful resources.

Summary of view B

Key words column:

Recent views of the function

differ considerably. One function attributed to the

Stuart Piddocke proposes that

Therefore, according to Piddocke

Suttles ... has an almost identical view

He believes

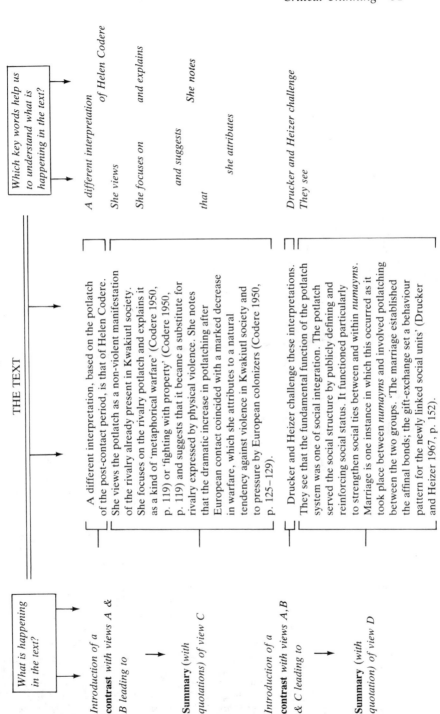

Which key words help us to understand what is happening in the text?

A different interpretation .... of Helen Codere

She views

She focuses on .... and explains

.... and suggests .... She notes

that .... She notes

.... she attributes

Drucker and Heizer challenge
They see

THE TEXT

A different interpretation, based on the potlatch of the post-contact period, is that of Helen Codere. She views the potlatch as a non-violent manifestation of the rivalry already present in Kwakiutl society. She focuses on the rivalry potlatch and explains it as a kind of 'metaphorical warfare' (Codere 1950, p. 119) or 'fighting with property' (Codere 1950, p. 119) and suggests that it became a substitute for rivalry expressed by physical violence. She notes that the dramatic increase in potlatching after European contact coincided with a marked decrease in warfare, which she attributes to a natural tendency against violence in Kwakiutl society and to pressure by European colonizers (Codere 1950, p. 125–129).

Drucker and Heizer challenge these interpretations. They see that the fundamental function of the potlatch system was one of social integration. The potlatch served the social structure by publicly defining and reinforcing social status. It functioned particularly to strengthen social ties between and within *numayms*. Marriage is one instance in which this occurred as it took place between *numayms* and involved potlatching between the two groups. 'The marriage established the affinal bonds; the gift-exchange set a behaviour pattern for the newly linked social units' (Drucker and Heizer 1967, p. 152).

What is happening in the text?

Introduction of a **contrast** with views A & B leading to

Summary (with quotations) of view C

Introduction of a **contrast** with views A, B & C leading to

Summary (with quotation) of view D

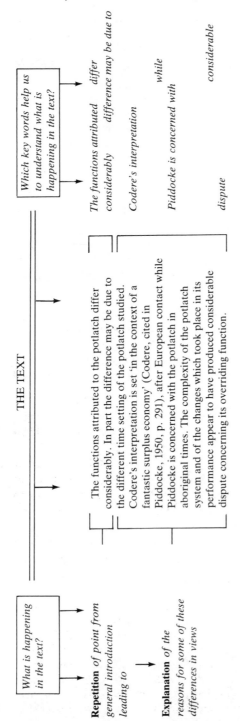

in which she attempts to discuss various interpretations. Read only the text of the essay, ignoring for the moment the words in the margins.

Now take note of what is written in the margins. In the left-hand margin we describe what the student is doing: is she summarizing one of the interpretations? comparing and contrasting one with another? pointing out strengths and weaknesses of particular interpretations? making a judgement about the relative worth of different interpretations?

In the right-hand margin we select those **key words** from the essay which identify what the student is doing at each stage. They are signposts to guide the reader through the text — a kind of code that reveals the pattern of the student's thinking. Thus phrases like 'She notes that ...', 'she attributes ...', 'He believes ...' tell us that the student is **summarizing** another writer's argument. On the other hand, 'differences may be due to ...' suggests a tentative **judgement** by the student in which she tries to explain why the interpretations are different.

Go back now and read the text again, including what is written in the margins. Notice particularly where the writer is summarizing and where she is making judgements.

What did you notice? That most of the marginal comments and the key words had to do with **summarizing** different writers' views? That, apart from the last paragraph, there was almost no questioning or judgement from the student?

In fact the student was praised by her lecturer for defining her terms clearly, for making an accurate summary of the different views, and for making some attempt to relate the different views to one another (comparison and contrast). She lost marks, however, for her failure to be sufficiently critical, i.e. to question the value of different interpretations and come to some overall judgement about them. Look at part of the comment which the lecturer made on her essay:

> ... In drawing comparisons and contrasts, you have failed to go on to the next step and say what the problems are with each interpretation. You state, for instance, that some of your sources 'challenge' the interpretations offered by other anthropologists, but you never tell us whether you think it is a convincing challenge, or a successful one ... you simply place the two views side by side and leave the reader to draw his own conclusion. In the last paragraph you do try to explain why two of the interpretations are different, i.e. they were dealing

with different periods of tribal development, but you never try to come to any conclusion about which is the most satisfactory explanation, i.e. the one which, in your judgement, best fits the evidence.

If you look back to the four criteria for the assessment of essays that we set out on p. 38, you can judge for yourself how this essay would be assessed. It would receive good marks on Criterion 1 (clear focus on the set topic) and Criterion 4 (competent presentation). But it would be marked down on Criterion 2 (for lack of 'critical' reading) and most of all on Criterion 3 (the presentation of a 'reasoned argument').

A **reasoned argument** is the outcome of critical thinking. That is, after reading, questioning, thinking, the student should reach a judgement about the value of different interpretations of views and then set out to **prove** that judgement. The essay then becomes not just a summary of facts and ideas, but a case which is argued and justified. A good essay **makes use of** facts and ideas rather than simply records them.

We can see what this distinction between summary and argument means in practice by looking at an extract from one of the anthropological sources that the student herself used in her essay: the book by the anthropologists Drucker and Heizer, who believe that the primary function of the potlatch is to promote social integration. We have chosen an extract in which the authors deal with a contrasting view to their own argument.

As you read, notice the way the authors use facts and ideas to argue their case. Notice how they go beyond mere comparison and contrast and make judgements about the value of the competing interpretation, pointing out its strengths and weaknesses. The ultimate purpose of their criticism, of course, is to prove that their own interpretation is the most satisfactory one.

We suggest you proceed in the same way as before:

Read only the text in the first reading; then go back to the beginning and read again, this time stopping to take note of the comments and key words set out in the margins.
(See extract on pages 55–58.)

Did you notice how much of this text — in contrast to the student's essay — is devoted to establishing the strengths and weaknesses of a rival interpretation? To making distinctions and judgements? Certainly there are passages in which the authors suspend their argument momentarily in order to summarize Codere's

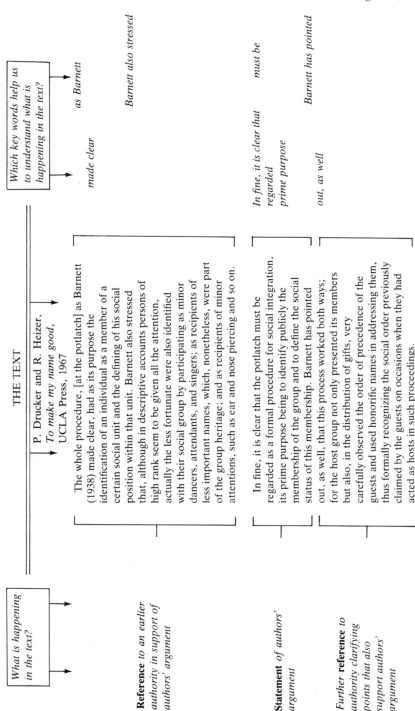

Which key words help us to understand what is happening in the text?

made clear   as Barnett

Barnett also stressed

In fine, it is clear that   must be
regarded
prime purpose

out, as well   Barnett has pointed

THE TEXT

P. Drucker and R. Heizer,
To make my name good,
UCLA Press, 1967

The whole procedure, [at the potlatch] as Barnett (1938) made clear, had as its purpose the identification of an individual as a member of a certain social unit and the defining of his social position within that unit. Barnett also stressed that, although in descriptive accounts persons of high rank seem to be given all the attention, actually the less fortunate were also identified with their social group by participating as minor dancers, attendants, and singers; as recipients of less important names, which, nonetheless, were part of the group heritage; and as recipients of minor attentions, such as ear and nose piercing and so on.

In fine, it is clear that the potlatch must be regarded as a formal procedure for social integration, its prime purpose being to identify publicly the membership of the group and to define the social status of this membership. Barnett has pointed out, as well, that this process worked both ways; for the host group not only presented its members but also, in the distribution of gifts, very carefully observed the order of precedence of the guests and used honorific names in addressing them, thus formally recognizing the social order previously claimed by the guests on occasions when they had acted as hosts in such proceedings.

What is happening in the text?

Reference to an earlier authority in support of authors' argument

Statement of authors' argument

Further **reference** to authority clarifying points that also support authors' argument

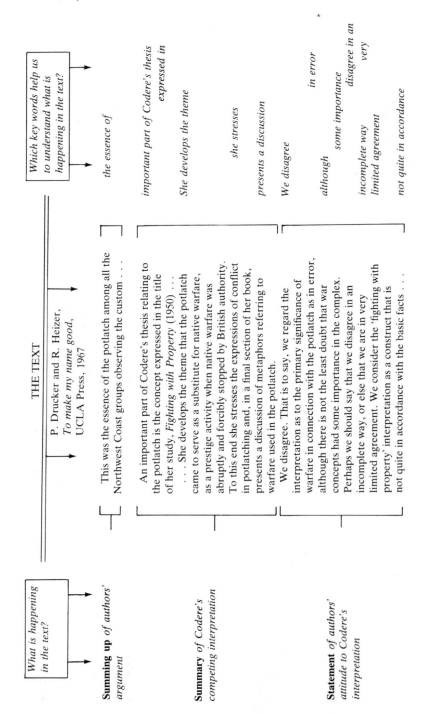

Which key words help us to understand what is happening in the text?

the essence of

important part of Codere's thesis expressed in

She develops the theme

she stresses

presents a discussion

We disagree

although   *in error*

some importance

disagree in an   *very*

incomplete way

limited agreement

not quite in accordance

THE TEXT

P. Drucker and R. Heizer,
To make my name good,
UCLA Press, 1967

This was the essence of the potlatch among all the Northwest Coast groups observing the custom . . . .

An important part of Codere's thesis relating to the potlatch is the concept expressed in the title of her study, *Fighting with Property* (1950) . . . . . . She develops the theme that the potlatch came to serve as a substitute for native warfare, as a prestige activity when native warfare was abruptly and forcibly stopped by British authority. To this end she stresses the expressions of conflict in potlatching and, in a final section of her book, presents a discussion of metaphors referring to warfare used in the potlatch.

We disagree. That is to say, we regard the interpretation as to the primary significance of warfare in connection with the potlatch as in error, although there is not the least doubt that war concepts had some importance in the complex. Perhaps we should say that we disagree in an incomplete way, or else that we are in very limited agreement. We consider the 'fighting with property' interpretation as a construct that is not quite in accordance with the basic facts . . .

What is happening in the text?

Summing up *of authors' argument*

Summary *of Codere's competing interpretation*

Statement *of authors' attitude to Codere's interpretation*

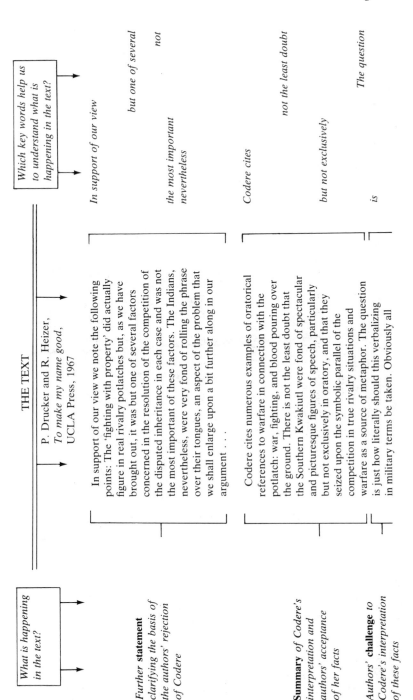

THE TEXT

P. Drucker and R. Heizer,
To make my name good,
UCLA Press, 1967

What is happening in the text?

Further **statement** *clarifying the basis of the authors' rejection of Codere*

In support of our view we note the following points: The 'fighting with property' did actually figure in real rivalry potlatches but, as we have brought out, it was but one of several factors concerned in the resolution of the competition of the disputed inheritance in each case and was not the most important of these factors. The Indians, nevertheless, were very fond of rolling the phrase over their tongues, an aspect of the problem that we shall enlarge upon a bit further along in our argument . . .

Summary *of Codere's interpretation and authors' acceptance of her facts*

Codere cites numerous examples of oratorical references to warfare in connection with the potlatch: war, fighting, and blood pouring over the ground. There is not the least doubt that the Southern Kwakiutl were fond of spectacular and picturesque figures of speech, particularly but not exclusively in oratory, and that they seized upon the symbolic parallel of the competition in true rivalry situations and

Authors' **challenge** *to Codere's interpretation of these facts*

warfare as a source of metaphor. The question is just how literally should this verbalizing in military terms be taken. Obviously all

Which key words help us to understand what is happening in the text?

In support of our view

but one of several

not

the most important
nevertheless

Codere cites

not the least doubt

but not exclusively

The question

is

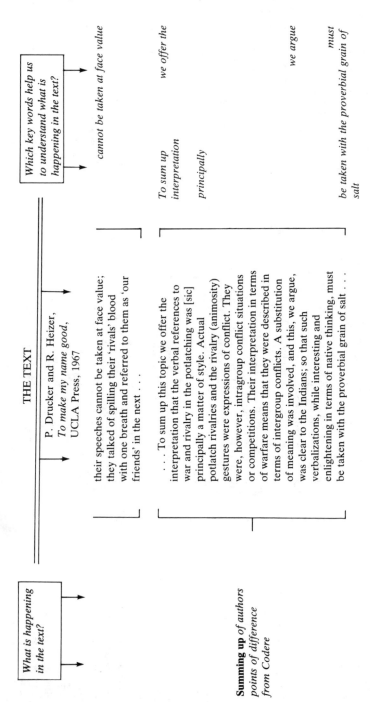

What is happening in the text?

THE TEXT

P. Drucker and R. Heizer,
To make my name good,
UCLA Press, 1967

their speeches cannot be taken at face value; they talked of spilling their 'rivals' blood with one breath and referred to them as 'our friends' in the next . . .

. . . To sum up this topic we offer the interpretation that the verbal references to war and rivalry in the potlatching was [sic] principally a matter of style. Actual potlatch rivalries and the rivalry (animosity) gestures were expressions of conflict. They were, however, intragroup conflict situations or competitions. Their interpretation in terms of warfare means that they were described in terms of intergroup conflicts. A substitution of meaning was involved, and this, we argue, was clear to the Indians; so that such verbalizations, while interesting and enlightening in terms of native thinking, must be taken with the proverbial grain of salt . . .

Which key words help us to understand what is happening in the text?

cannot be taken at face value

To sum up
interpretation

principally

we offer the

we argue

must
be taken with the proverbial grain of salt

Summing up *of authors points of difference from Codere* interpretation, but only for the purpose of then arguing a point in relation to that summary. The summary by itself is of limited value; what matters is the way in which the authors use that summary to help build their own argument. As the authors themselves say at another point in the same article: 'We shall therefore use his [another scholar's] work as a springboard to clarify our views.'

This distinction between the processes of **summary** and of **argument** may be made clearer if we look at the way each text has handled the same subject: Codere's interpretation of the function of the potlatch. The relevant passage from the student's essay is paragraph 3

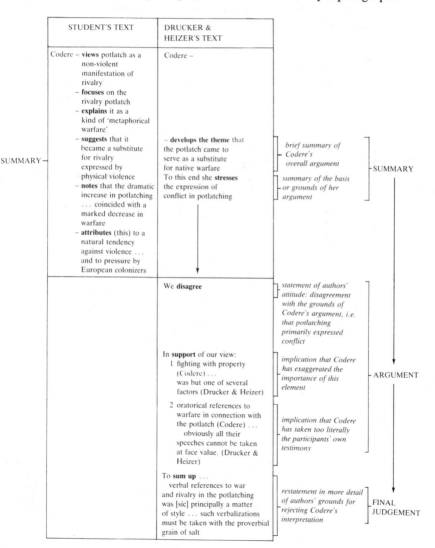

beginning with the words 'A different interpretation ...' and from Drucker and Heizer's text the section beginning 'An important part of Codere's thesis ...' Look quickly at those passages now to remind yourself of their content and then examine the analysis on page 59.

As you can see at a glance the weight and emphasis in the student's text is on summary and in Drucker and Heizer's text on argument. They do use summary in places but only as a 'springboard' for the development of their own argument. During her undergraduate career our student writer will be expected to move gradually from the summary approach she is presently adopting to the critical approach displayed in the sources she uses.

Summary

In this chapter we have tried to show what is meant by **critical thinking** in relation to tertiary study. It consists
first, in **analysis**:
- reducing a complex matter to its simple elements,
- examining the relationships among them;
then, in adopting a **critical** attitude towards those elements:
- questioning their meaning,
- evaluating the evidence for them,
- making judgements about their value or importance; and
finally, in presenting those judgements in a persuasive and reasoned **argument**.

This approach involves a shift away from the simpler practices of recording and summarizing which are common in secondary school. Summary may still be necessary at times, but it will be brief and used only to provide the basis for developing a critical argument.

We have made an important qualification to these general statements in relation to Science and Technology courses. Here the emphasis may be heavily on summary and analysis in the early stages of a course, with criticism becoming a requirement only in later years.

MORE TO THINK ABOUT

1 Make a list of the five most important influences on your educational achievement up to the present. (It might include items such as encouragement by a relative or the example of a particular teacher.)

Then, under each of your five headings, write two or three sentences which **describe** in more detail the effects of this influence.

Now **analyse** the varying importance of these five factors upon you and then write a final **evaluation** of these influences in order to explain why you are now hoping to study abroad.

2 Take any chapter from a textbook or any article from an academic journal which you are presently using for study in your school or university. It can be either in English or in your own language. Read three or four pages, making a note at the end of each paragraph of what the writer is doing:
  • is he simply presenting factual information?
  • is he summarizing other writers' ideas or theories?
  • is he comparing and contrasting the information or ideas with those of another writer?
  • is he arguing his own particular interpretation of the facts?
  • is he criticizing the ideas of other writers?
  • is he doing a number of these things in one paragraph?

Now take an article from a newspaper or a magazine such as *Time* or *Newsweek* and, in the same way, analyse what the writer is doing in each paragraph.

Compare your notes for each piece of writing and then discuss with a fellow student how far the different **purposes** of each writer have determined the different patterns of presentation.

3 Appendix 5 contains an extract from a Biology textbook in which the author is discussing the relationship between the behaviour of animals and the breadth of their habitat.

Read the entire extract carefully. Then, following the pattern we adopted for the other texts in this chapter, write in the right-hand margin those **key words** which help you to understand what is happening in the text.

Compare your results with a fellow student and then with the full class. After you have isolated the key words, discuss together the comments that might go in the left-hand margin. (Is the author **summarizing** the present state of knowledge? Is she **providing evidence** for or against that view? Is she **establishing the reasons** for uncertainty in the evidence? Is she **drawing a conclusion** about the evidence?)

You might also go on to compare the style of argument in this passage with that in the passage from Drucker and Heizer (pp. 55–58). In what ways are they similar? In what ways are they both different from the anthropology student's writing (pp. 50–52)?

Chapter 6
Strategies for Undergraduate Studies

All students are different. They have different capabilities, different motivations and different ways of studying. So no single system of study will suit everyone. Nor is there — as you will already know yourself — any one strategy or magic formula which will automatically ensure success.

Nevertheless, from our work with students, we have found there are some strategies for study which, used flexibly, do seem more helpful than no strategies at all. They cover the problems we have already mentioned in earlier chapters: (1) time management, (2) lectures and note-taking, (3) tutorials and lab sessions, (4) reading and library research, (5) written assignments, and (6) revision and exams. We shall now look at each of these in turn, drawing on the experience of both overseas and Australian students. Our purpose is to suggest ways in which you may avoid unnecessary strain in adjusting to study abroad.

1 Time management

Some students find they work more efficiently if they can set out for themselves a detailed daily and weekly study timetable for a whole term or semester. They allot regular periods for all rest and leisure activities as well as plotting hourly study sessions. This approach to time management follows the pattern familiar from secondary school. It seems to be a common strategy among Science and Technology students whose study is dominated by lectures and lab sessions and is, therefore, predictable. Yet this predictability can also cause problems. If, for example, some unexpected event occurs — maybe sickness or the need to repeat an unsatisfactory experiment — then the whole scheme appears to be in ruins, and much time and effort can be wasted in drawing up a revised but equally rigid schedule.

Most students find, in practice, that they cannot keep to such detailed hour-by-hour timetables. A lab report may take less time to write up than was anticipated, but some Maths problem may take a lot longer to solve. Moreover, you will certainly find that the amount of work required for each course varies from week to week. Some weeks you may only be required to attend lectures and to do a couple of hours additional study. Other weeks, when a major essay or a report on a complex experiment is due, you may need to spend most of your time on this work and almost totally neglect work for your other courses. Unlike the regular patterns of high school learning, university study has very uneven rhythms. Some first-year students complain that the academic year starts gently with four weeks of relatively little pressure, and thereafter it is eight months of perpetual crisis.

So some form of planning does seem useful. In fact we suggest it is useful to use two styles of planning: one which is **time-centred** and maps out your fixed commitments and deadlines, and one which is **task-centred** and brings some order into your independent study time. For the first few weeks of the year you will need a weekly timetable to remind yourself of fixed commitments such as lectures, labs and tutorials, sports practices, club meetings and so on. This schedule will soon become so familiar, as the weeks go by, that you won't need to look at it very often. But it is also useful to draw up a longer-range plan, maybe covering a month, or a term, in which you plot out the important deadlines for assignments, tests, holiday dates and other commitments that fall within this period.

The illustration on page 64 is one example of such a plan. It covers a period of five weeks (the second half of one term) and was constructed by a Science undergraduate who was studying second-year Maths, Physics, Chemistry, plus an optional course in Science German. The shaded area at the end of each week indicates the day he set aside for sport and social activities.

On the basis of your long-range plan, you can then begin to make decisions about which particular tasks need to be started and which must be completed within each coming week. This task-centred approach seems much more useful than the sort of rigid hour-by-hour schedule we described earlier. Your planning can often develop from such questions as 'What do I need to get through by the end of the week? What parts of which courses are particularly hard and require more time? Do I need to get an early start on revision for a test or reading for an assignment not due till next month?' Many students find it more realistic and helpful to plan that 'by the end of this week I will finish my Economics worksheets and my reading for my Accounting essay' rather than scheduling 'I shall spend two hours on Monday and Wednesday on Economics and two

WEEK 1 | 2 | 3 | 4 | 5 | END of TERM

HOLIDAY — VISIT FAMILY

Maths assignment Due Sheets |——→ *

Start revision *   Due |——→ *

Practise exam problems *

Maths exam * →   Due |——→ *   Test

Start reading for Physics assignment *

Start experiments *

Write up *

Write up 2nd draft Submit * ——→ *

2nd draft Submit * ——→ *

Start Chem experiment for major Project *

hour   each morning

Start revision for exam *

Practise on past papers * ——→ *   Test

Science German ½ *

Hockey Training Tu & Th *

Film Club Weds. 7.30pm *

hours on Tuesday and Thursday in the library reading for my Accounting course'. Often you may get to the library according to your schedule, only to find all the Accounting books you need have already been borrowed by another student . . .

When developing a task-centred timetable, you should review it regularly, maybe at the end of each week. You need to consider what you actually did achieve in the past week. How effective was the way you spent your time? Too little or too much time spent preparing for tutorials — or writing up lecture notes? Should you have spent more time in the lab and less in the library — or the other way round? Was the time spent on writing reports justified in terms of the grades you received? In the light of this kind of assessment you can then plan the coming week more realistically.

If you find you are falling behind seriously in your work, then you may be wise to seek the advice of a counsellor or academic adviser at the university. Inexperienced students frequently complain along these lines: 'I really revised for that test all week. I dropped all my other courses, and I stayed up two nights going over my lecture notes. And still I only scrapped through with a Pass.' It is not only the amount of time that you spend studying that matters; it is the effectiveness and quality of your study that really counts. If your studying is not producing satisfactory results, you may need more help than just a good system of timetabling.

Pressure from lack of time is often a particular problem for students from overseas. Because of the problems with English, including local accents and academic style, you will inevitably have to allow more time than native speakers of English for coping with reading and for producing essays and reports. You may find the only way to do this is to cut back on leisure activities, or work longer hours than the average local student. Such tactics are unavoidable, at least in the early months of your degree course when you are adjusting to many new demands.

It is important, however, to change your study habits as your familiarity with the language and methods of study develops. Some overseas students fall into the trap of believing that if they spend a lot of time studying and if they memorize all their materials, then they will succeed in their courses. This is seldom the most effective approach at any level of tertiary studies.

Our general advice on time management, therefore, would be this: try not to let time dominate your thinking and so force you into rigid planning and timetabling. A rigid schedule is not appropriate to the varying demands that face you over the course of an academic year.

2 Lectures and note-taking

In Australian universities lectures are never the only source of information about a course; nor are they a sufficient source on their
own. So trying to take down immensely detailed notes in lectures is
not necessarily a good strategy for study.

In some courses, as in Science, first-year lectures follow the sequence of a textbook or work manual; they expand, explain and develop the text. For such courses you are expected to buy all the
relevant textbooks, as prescribed by the lecturer, and read the relevant section before each lecture. Then you do not need to take
detailed notes during the lecture but merely put down the key points
and any additional explanations or examples which help to throw
light on the text. In other courses the lectures may be a way of
teaching a process, rather than imparting content. For example, in
Law the lecture may be a practical demonstration of the way to read
and analyse a case, or in Forestry how to measure timber product
from a stand of trees. In other courses, such as Biochemistry or History, the lectures may raise a variety of different theories about cell
structures or conflicting interpretations of an historical event. In
such cases one major objective of the lecturer is to direct you to a
range of books and articles in which you can follow some of these
controversies in more detail. In lectures of this type you need to listen attentively, making notes on important ideas and key references
which you must work on later in your own time. So there is no single strategy for coping with lectures and no single method of note-
taking which is effective for all situations. As always, you must
adjust your strategy to each new situation.

As local students become more experienced and more confident
in their studies, they adapt their responses to lectures according to
their own purposes. If the lectures are central to the coverage and
understanding of the material in the course, then they plan to attend
them regularly. If they miss a lecture, they try to borrow notes from
a friend or, if the lecture has been recorded on tape, they arrange to
listen to the tape in the audio-visual centre or wherever it is made
available for students to use. In some courses a student may decide
to skip a lecture if he is under pressure to complete an assignment.
Missing a lecture is much more common than missing a tutorial or
lab session, and it is more common in courses where the content of
the lectures is at least partly available in a textbook or some other
source, such as notes provided by the lecturer himself. In many lectures the experienced student takes only a couple of pages of notes
in the whole hour. These may consist merely of phrases or single
words to remind him of the points the lecturer has raised. His

concentration during the lecture goes into thinking about the implications of the points raised by the lecturer, rather than trying to record them word for word. Most lecturers approve of this approach to note-taking and disapprove of students who attempt to get down every word they say.

Lecture notes, therefore, are guidelines. They may later be expanded by notes from other reading or experiments, by ideas raised in tutorials, and by your own reflections on the course content.

Overseas students often find particular problems in comprehending what is being said in a lecture and simultaneously taking notes. Here is an Indonesian undergraduate commenting on her initial experience in a foreign university:

> When I first started my undergraduate education I was not always able to understand what the lectures were about... In the beginning I had to concentrate very hard on the language, which I had to translate into my mother-tongue. However, by doing so I often missed the subject being discussed. Then, in some cases, the subject of the courses I was required to attend was completely unfamiliar to me because I come from Indonesia. The combination of the two often led to a situation where at the end of the lecture period my notebook was empty. However, on hindsight, this was not only due to the language and the subject matter, but also, and probably more so, due to my inability to take notes from lectures. My past secondary education in Indonesia did not prepare me for such a skill. We used to be given notes by the teachers, which were either handed out or which we diligently copied during the class time.

This student has raised two problems: first, following the lecture and making notes; second, lack of background knowledge common to local students. Here is a Hong Kong student commenting on the first of these problems:

> I find it very hard to both listen, absorb and write at the same time. Very often I find I don't get what the lecturer is trying to convey at the instant he finished his sentence and the next moment he's going on to something else. I do feel sometimes that I'm more a recording machine (trying to write down most of the things the lecturer said) than trying to get the essence of the lecture.

You may find it possible to overcome this problem initially by making use of the tapes of lectures in your own time. If a lecturer does not regularly make tapes of his lectures, then you must ask his permission to sit in the front row and tape it yourself with your own cassette recorder. Most lecturers will permit this so long as they have been asked in advance and so long as the tape is for your personal use. Overseas students have found this strategy extremely helpful, until they reach a stage of sufficient fluency in English to be able to follow the lecture.

The second problem raised by the Indonesian student, her lack of common background with other students, is more difficult. In part it can only be overcome gradually as you read more, learn more about the local background, and come to understand more of the daily life and concerns of the society. Another Hong Kong student makes this point in relation to an introductory course in Sociology:

> I find the lectures interesting and systematic. However, I have some difficulties in following the discussion. This, I think, is mostly due to my lack of knowledge about Western society and culture which provide the basic foundations for studying Sociology (with respect to a Western country like Australia). Therefore, at times I really wonder whether I am just digging the surface of the discipline while others are drilling at its core.

3 Tutorials and laboratory sessions

Tutorials and labs provide you with an opportunity to try out your own ideas and develop your experimental skills. One important difference between these two types of practical classes lies in the way in which you use out-of-class time. The benefit you get from a tutorial depends greatly on the work you have done **before** the tutorial meeting: reading about the topic to be covered, turning over in your mind the key issues and problems, maybe speculating on the points likely to be raised and the questions that must be answered. Preparation for lab sessions may be less important; the more important independent work **follows** the session when you reflect on the methods of the experiment, the findings, and the significance of these, and then write up your lab report.

The most significant point they have in common is the necessity for you to be actively involved in the tutorial discussion or experiment. In Indonesia there is a sarcastic way of referring to easy-going courses as requiring only the six D's: **D**atang (to come), **D**aftar (to register), **D**uduk (to sit), **D**engar (to listen), **D**iam (to be silent), and **D**uit (to get paid allowances). Such an approach to labs and tutorials would produce little effective learning. If you are poorly prepared to join in the work, or too shy to take part in the discussion, or hesitant to ask questions about points you do not understand, or reluctant to answer questions and risk being wrong, then much of the value of the session, both for you and your fellow students, is wasted.

Participation in tutorials and labs can be terrifying at first for overseas students unaccustomed to this style of learning. Our Indonesian student again sets out her own experience:

> At first, attending seminars and discussion groups was a nightmare because class participation determined part of the grades. First of all, in high school I had been trained to be a passive recipient. Teachers were not to be questioned, I was not to air my views, and never was class discussion allowed. Then, in college, I had to say something in class. That in itself was a difficult hurdle to overcome. But, on top of it, I was very unsure of myself about my comprehension of the reading assignment. Moreover, I was not used to presenting arguments and I did not know how to reply to challenges. Basically, I was afraid to sound stupid in front of my classmates. I would have been ashamed and would not know how to behave.

An African student describes another very common feeling:

> It takes time for an overseas student to take part in tutorials — at first all he does is to study other students contributing to the discussions.

Finally, a Chinese student points out a cultural problem in his attitude to public argument:

> The seminars and group discussions always upset me, especially when everyone tries to argue on a certain topic. I find it hard to concentrate on the whole discussion and hence very seldom can I enter into the argument at all.

With time, however, most overseas students do manage to overcome their reluctance to join in these practical sessions. Here is the way a Thai student tackled the problem:

> At first I did not speak at all. Everyone else speaks so fast and I didn't want to interrupt, speaking slowly and holding up the discussion. Then I got my plan. Each week before the tutorial I read the articles on the subject and write down some opinions in English about it. I learn them and when everyone else is quiet, I can give my idea, speaking almost as fast as my classmates. This gives me confidence. Then one day I could state my ideas without writing it down — it just came out. I still have a problem when they ask me questions. But it is getting easier now.

Other foreign students use a different strategy: they invite some classmates to meet for an 'unofficial' tutorial before the official session. In this more relaxed and friendly setting they can practise their ideas. Here they need not worry that they might be delaying the rest of the class or sounding stupid. After these practice tutorials, these students claim it is then much easier to answer questions and put forward ideas in the real group discussions.

4 Reading and library research

The amount of reading which is expected in most courses, and especially in Arts and Social Science courses, presents difficulties for many students. At school students were accustomed to reading only two or three short chapters for their regular assignments. Suddenly they find they are expected to work their way through much more extensive and much more difficult reading every week for tutorials and essays. They complain, 'There is too much to get through. I end up reading it all with my eyes but nothing is going into my head. I read it so slowly it takes hours to finish even one article. And then I can't remember what it was all about, so I have to start all over again!'

Also, in many courses there are frustrating problems in getting hold of the recommended books and articles in the library. In a large course with four hundred students there are seldom sufficient copies of key books to meet the sudden demand before an essay deadline. Such books are usually only available for restricted borrowing in a Short Loan system; you may only borrow the book for a short period, usually two hours, and may not take it out of the library. So you need to develop reading strategies which make it possible to get the main points from a book within a very limited time. You must also develop a method for making notes which can be used later for your essay or tutorial.

And in all university courses you need to read critically. This means learning to recognize and select the information that is relevant to your purpose. Are you reading to gather specific facts for a report or essay? Are you reading to check that there are no alternative theories or interpretations to challenge your argument? Are you looking for useful quotations? Or legal precedents in law reports? Critical reading, then, is only possible if you have a clear **purpose** for your reading.

Many students complain that they read too slowly. There are books about speed reading and systems for reading more effectively — some are less useful than others. Some promise miracles. In our experience, miracles seldom happen. We consider most speed reading courses are not really appropriate to academic studies, however useful they may be in secondary school or in business or administration. At university the most important consideration is understanding the content and selecting the relevant points for your own purpose; speed of reading, without comprehension, is of little value.

We find the most useful strategy for academic reading is to develop some system for **skimming** a piece of writing in order to gain, from the start, a general view of the argument and material the writer is presenting. This can be done, with most academic texts, in the following way:

a Read the **opening paragraph** of the chapter or article — this usually sets out the main topic to be covered.

b Read **only the first sentences** of the paragraphs that follow.

c Read the whole **final paragraph** — this commonly sums up the argument.

Occasionally, depending on the author's style, it may be necessary to read the final sentence of each paragraph instead of, or as well as, the opening sentence. If the book makes use of headings, tables, illustrations or any other clues to understanding the body of the text, these are useful guidelines for skimming.

The main advantage in using this style of skimming is that you gain an overview of the whole text first. On the basis of this you can then decide whether, for **your** purpose, i.e. the purpose of your essay, tutorial paper or test, you need to read the whole chapter or only one section, whether you need to take notes, whether the writer's argument is useful. This cuts out much unnecessary reading.

Overseas students find the emphasis on independent reading a particular burden. Many have come from education systems with poor library resources, and so extensive reading is a new activity. Moreover, if they are not confident in their command of English, quick and critical reading seems a risky business: 'What if I miss some important points?' Our Indonesian student once again voices this worry:

> There were several reasons why reading assignments were difficult. Again they are related to both the language and the subject. Focusing on the language, I would say that the first stumbling block was my limited vocabulary. However, finding meanings of particular words does not guarantee understanding of a sentence and paragraph. Then, neither did I know how to read a book, a chapter in a book, or an article. The skill of reading for content only was already very difficult, but it was more difficult for critical reading. I was only taught that the written word was the 'truth'. I had no experience in searching for weaknesses and criticizing other people's work. To complicate matters, the reading assignments were enormous by my past experiences. In high school we mostly only used one text-book for a course, which

lasted for one year. In college I was suddenly faced by the fact that we had to read several books and articles. I often did not know where to start and how to select what to skim and what to read more carefully.

Again this problem stems partly from a lack of fluency in English and partly from a different approach to learning — the shift from 'the written word as truth' to the printed word as a tool for your own use.

You will find that, although you may never quite achieve the ease in reading of a native English speaker, you will gradually increase your speed and your comprehension. At first you may have to work slowly with dictionaries: a dictionary of English and your own language for general vocabulary; an advanced English dictionary for more complex definitions; and a specialist dictionary (for example, a Dictionary of Earth Science or a Dictionary of Legal Terms) for the technical language you need in each discipline. Eventually this close attention to meaning pays dividends. You may even find that you end up with a more accurate grasp of special terminology and phrases than many local students.

5 Written assignments

The most severe problems local students face are related to their written assignments. Whether it is a lab report, an essay, a research project or a sub-thesis, they find it hard to express their ideas on paper and frustrating to write under pressure of deadlines. As English is their own language, fluency is unlikely to be a major problem; it is the quality of their thinking and the effectiveness of the way they manage to present it that provide the challenge. And, as we have seen in the previous chapter, the process of developing an argument in writing is demanding.

The stages of producing an assignment, in particular an essay, are extremely complex and can only be summarized here.[1] Most students who become accomplished in writing essays work through some variation of the following stages:

a *analysing the topic*: This involves reading the set topic with close attention to

---

[1] For a complete account of these stages, and a demonstration of the process of skimming referred to in the previous section, see the authors' text: J. Clanchy & B. Ballard, *Essay Writing for Students*, Longman Cheshire, Melbourne, 1981 (reprinted as *How to Write Essays* (International edition), Longman Cheshire, Melbourne, 1983).

the **content** indicated,
the **focus** required,
the **issue** to be determined, and
the **method** to be used in the essay.

Look, for example, at this Zoology topic:

> '*By any standards, the insect body must be reckoned the most successful of all the solutions to the problems of living on the surface of the earth.*' (*Attenborough, 1979*) *Discuss this statement, critically, basing your discussion on evidence.*

In analysing this topic you must decide upon:

the general area of content	— insect physiology and morphology
the particular focus	— adaptation of the insect body to life on earth
the issue to be determined	— is the insect body 'the most successful' adaptation?
the method to be used	— evidence drawn from insect and other animal species.

So now you realize you are not being asked to write a general essay on insects or even the insect body. You are being asked to make a judgement about degrees of adaptation, evaluating the success of insects against that of other animals. So your reading, and your essay, will focus on the problem of defining 'successful' adaptation to life on earth, using insects and other animal species for evidence.

Do you remember, from Chapter 4, the first criterion lecturers use in assessing an essay: *It is expected that the essay will be clearly focused on the set topic and will deal fully with its central concerns?* This first step of analysing the topic is a move towards meeting that expectation.

b *reading and note-taking*: The second criterion for assessing an essay was *It is expected that the essay will be the result of wide and critical reading.* This stage involves the systematic gathering, selecting and evaluating of the material that will eventually form the basis for your essay. In the process of researching for the essay, you go through the steps of skimming, reading closely, and taking notes selectively — always with the aim of collecting only those points which seem relevant to your topic.

While it is impossible to be specific about the amount of notes you should take for any particular assignment, the form in which these notes are made and stored should satisfy four basic criteria:

a Your notes must be **legible**.

b They must be kept in a **flexible** system. When you are writing an essay you will often need to rearrange items of information to suit the purposes of your analysis. Notes made on loose leaf paper or cards can be easily rearranged; notes made in bound exercise books or pads cannot.

c They must be **identifiable**. Each set of notes should be clearly identified with a heading that lists all of the bibliographic details of the book or article from which the notes were taken (author, title, place of publication, edition, date). This makes it easy for you to check details of fact and quotations with the original source when you write your assignment. It also makes it easy to construct the bibliography or list of references to sources which must be attached at the end of every essay.

d They should leave **room for comment**. Wide margins are useful. As you build up your notes you will want to add cross-references to other sources and some comments of your own.

Of course the amount of notes you take also depends upon the amount of reading you do. How much should you read? If you read too much or for too long, you will have to use more judgement at the writing stage: if you read too little, your essay may be criticized as 'thin'. Much depends on the course, the length of the assignment, the nature of the topic, and the resources available. Much also depends on how much time and effort you can spare for the task. One first-year course in Political Science provides students with an initial reading list of ten items for a 2000-word essay. The lecturer advises students to read a minimum of six to eight items (not whole books but selected chapters and articles) but warns that a good essay would require a lot more reading than this.

c *planning the essay*: Remember: *It is expected that the essay will present a reasoned argument.* In some assignments, such as lab reports or book reviews, the structure of the assignment is standard, so this step does not present any great problem. You may still have to decide which material to introduce first and how to develop points within a section; but the general structure is determined by the nature of the assignment.

In most essays, however, the effectiveness of the argument depends greatly on the way it is structured, so planning is important.

Some students prefer to make a fairly detailed plan of their whole essay before they start writing. Others prefer to map out only the general outline and then reorganize and develop their points as they write. Such students would explain that they do not find out what they think until they've tried to write it out; only then are they able to reorganize their ideas coherently. In general, then, some initial planning, if only of the steps of your argument, is usual. **At some stage in your writing** of the essay a coherent and satisfactory structure for your ideas must be developed.

d *writing the first drafts*: Even experienced and very competent students find it useful to write at least two drafts, or trial writings, of an essay. You may find you have to write three or four drafts before you have produced an essay that satisfies you. There is an important distinction between the first draft and later revisions. In the first writing you are still in the process of creating and finding out your own ideas on the topic; you gradually recognize the logic of your argument as you write. You may have to discard certain ideas and rewrite many sections before the whole argument really fits smoothly together. It is important to recognize that the initial draft is only an exploration, and the presentation is unlikely at this stage to be fluent and polished. In fact, if you do try to write 'perfectly' from the outset, you will probably get very frustrated. You will be trying to achieve perfection in each separate sentence when the whole flow of the essay is still far from clear. Much better, then, to regard the first draft as only a preliminary stage, a tentative start towards your final essay.

e *later drafts, editing and final draft*: If in your first draft you are developing your thoughts and your argument, in later drafts you are clarifying and reorganizing those initial thoughts into an effectively presented argument. Now your purpose is to **communicate** your ideas and argument to someone else — to your lecturer or your tutorial group — and you must deliberately shape your material for this purpose. If your essay is well-structured, your reader should be able to skim it — reading only your opening paragraph, the first sentences of later paragraphs, and your final paragraph — and gain a confident understanding of your ideas.

Finally, in order to satisfy the fourth criterion *It is expected that the essay will be competently presented*, you must edit the final draft very carefully for errors of style, format, grammar and spelling. Mistakes here spoil the total effect of the essay.

These, then, are the main stages through which all students go in producing an extended essay. You will go through very similar stages in writing a lab report but the process within each of these stages may vary. These variations result from those differences between an essay and a report that we pointed out in Chapter 4. Your reading, for example, is often brief and limited to basic principles; your note-taking is frequently restricted to observations on the experiment itself. The structure of a report is laid down firmly in advance, so you spend much less time in the planning and redrafting stages. Nevertheless some planning is required, particularly in the Introduction and Discussion sections where you must select and arrange ideas, facts and observations carefully. In the same way you must edit the final draft to meet the requirements of style and correctness that have been set out by the department.

For overseas students there may be additional difficulties relating to written English and to styles of argument and presentation, as we have seen in Chapter 2. The only way we know to improve your capacity to write essays is — to write more essays. And then to reflect on the ways in which your lecturer has graded and commented on your last essay, in order to improve your approach to the next one. Our Indonesian student summarized her writing problems mainly in terms of structure and approach to the task:

> The most obvious difficulties related to writing were of course grammar and vocabulary. Related to limitation on vocabulary is the ability to express and explain or describe ideas, situations or objects in a concise or extended manner as demanded. Furthermore, my cultural background and socialization process had conditioned my thinking process. This was reflected in the following ways. (1) There was often no theme running throughout my essay and it became instead a compilation of several unrelated ideas; (2) there was an inability to draw out similarities or patterns from a variety of identified individual properties; (3) there was an inability to present arguments in a logical and schematic fashion.

A Bangladesh student, who was working at Honours level, raised another problem common to overseas students:

> There is still one more difficulty that I come across time and time again, and I haven't found any solution to it as yet. When I am puzzled about a particular topic that I am writing on and when I have this pressure to hand the paper in by a certain date — sort of being in a position where you are being forced to write on something you have no interest in and you do not care about — I lose my ability to form correct English sentences. Somehow the words make sense to me but it gives me a headache thinking whether what I have written is correct English or not. It makes sense to me because I literally translate the sentence from my language to English; as a result the syntax gets all

wrong but my mind stops then and I become unsure of my whole argument.

Writing is always difficult if the material and the ideas you are trying to express are complex. This problem is not confined to overseas students. One Australian student complained: 'I know what I want to say but only 50% of it comes out on paper. Even then my lecturer can't understand what I'm getting at.' Yet this is an art which all students must develop, for so much of their progress and their future success depend on their skills in communicating their ideas in writing.

6 Exams and revision

A noticeable feature of many Asian education systems is the dominance of multiple-choice exams at all levels. Asian students gain a great deal of experience of exam competition in their school days and their undergraduate courses. Much of this training, however, is directed towards memorizing information and recognizing items on the test paper. These skills may not transfer very usefully to, say, the Australian and British systems. In these systems, with the exception of some Science courses, most exams require short or extended answers.

A common pattern for a three hour end-of-year exam in a Social Science course would be a paper requiring students to answer three out of six essay type questions. Here is an example of one question from an Accounting exam:

> *What are the major differences between a perpetual inventory system and a periodic inventory system? What general conditions lead to the use of one or other of the two systems by a company?*

And here is a question from a Political Science exam:

> *The view is often taken that legislatures have declined in importance. Do you agree with this view in relation to the Australian parliament?*

In some exams, such as Law, students may be permitted to bring all their textbooks and notes into the exam room with them. Exams of this kind — called 'open book exams' — test students' capacities to solve problems by applying the principles they have studied, rather than simply testing memory. In some courses there are no formal exams but students take home the exam paper for the weekend and work on it independently, handing their answers in to their lecturer three days later. So the variety of styles of examining may be confusing to you at first if you are only accustomed to multiple-choice tests.

The format of an exam determines, to some extent, the way in which you must revise for it. If you have a Science exam, where there may be multiple-choice questions as well as some written answers, then your revision may focus on facts and formulae, on re-production of theories and the results of experiments — generally on 'learning your notes'. If you are studying in Social Sciences or Arts, your exam will probably consist of essay questions and so your revision will concentrate on the **relationships** between facts and ideas rather than just on the facts and ideas themselves.

Some students claim they revise best in isolation, but many find that working in a study group, with three or four others, is more effective. In these groups they can go over old exam papers together for practice. They pool their knowledge and ideas. They discuss points of difficulty. They sharpen their skill in analysing questions quickly. They strengthen their confidence.

Even when students have revised effectively and know their material, they still face the problem, in the actual exam, of working against time. Inexperienced students often misjudge their time and spend too long on one question and too little on another, thus inevitably losing marks for the incomplete answers. Overseas students, struggling with language uncertainties, find time pressure particularly frustrating. Here is a Japanese student commenting on this problem:

> I found a formal exam extremely hard for me, because of language problem. Even if I do understand the words of the question, I just cannot put any ideas into English properly in the limited time of two or three hours. If it is optional, I definitely choose take-home exam or report or anything except a formal exam.

Conclusion

In this chapter we have covered some of the common strategies used by local and overseas students for coping with the demands of tertiary study. If this catalogue of problems and pitfalls has made you nervous about your own chances of success, listen to this list of problems which a Chinese student faced in her first year of study in Australia:

> Because of a lack of basic vocabulary I had some difficulties in follow-ing lectures, as well as in taking notes. I had no idea how to take notes for a start, and didn't know how to handle timetable and leisure time. It took rather a long time to get used to the libraries and when I

asked the staff behind the inquiry desk, I was never sure if I got what he meant. There was very little contact between me and my classmates in a big hall where the lectures were taking place. I was very slow in reading and writing. Meanwhile I doubted if my own notes could be of any use and was anxious how to catch up with others most of the time. When it's necessary to speak to the lecturers or tutors, I was conscious of my own awkward way in expressing myself, and was worried about assessment and final marks from an early time. There always were problems in essay writing and in understanding what our teachers' expectations were. I was not sure how to prepare for tutorials, and had many difficulties in giving a seminar orally.

With all these problems, you might expect that this student failed. Not at all — she managed to adapt to the new system and finished up as an Honours student in her two major subjects. And that Indonesian student whom we quoted so regularly in this chapter not only became an Honours student but finally gained her PhD in Australia and is now a lecturer in her own country. So these difficulties **can** be overcome . . .

Summary

Here we have outlined some of the learning strategies used by experienced students from both Australia and overseas. These strategies deal with problems relating to
 • time management,
 • lectures and note-taking,
 • tutorials and lab sessions,
 • reading and library research,
 • the process of writing essays and lab reports, and
 • exams and revision.
In each case special attention is given to the particular difficulties of students studying in a foreign country.

MORE TO THINK ABOUT

1 Over the next month, experiment with different approaches to planning your time. For each week draw up a **time-oriented** hour-by-hour timetable of what you hope to do for the following seven days. At the end of each week assess how realistic, or useful, this method of planning proved.

At the same time draw up a **task-oriented** plan for the next month, using the principles we described in the first section of this chapter (see p. 64 for an example of this style of planning). Then assess it in the same way, and compare the advantages and disadvantages of each approach.

2 In section 4 of this chapter we described a method of skimming in order to obtain a **quick outline of the argument** in a piece of writing. Try this technique for yourself.

Start with an extract (a chapter or sub-section) from a school or university textbook, written in English, about a subject you are studying. Skim it in the way we suggested:
   - read the opening paragraph in full,
   - then read the first sentence of each subsequent paragraph, and
   - read the final paragraph in full.

Were you able to follow the structure of the writer's argument? Would it help if you also read the final sentence of each paragraph?

If possible work with a partner who is also skimming the same extract. On the basis of your skimming, try to give him or her a quick summary of the passage. Then discuss those clues from the passage which you used to make up your summary and the points at which your summaries are different.

(Try practising this skimming method at least once a week.)

3 In the previous chapter we presented a long extract by the anthropologists Drucker and Heizer (pp. 55–58), and in Appendix 5 another extract by the biologist Partridge. Work together with a fellow student, each on a different extract. Make notes on the extracts in order to explain the writer's argument in a five minute oral presentation. (Try as far as possible to use your own wording.)

Make your presentation to your partner and ask him or her to comment on how clear your talk was.

Then discuss in the larger group any difficulties that arose in carrying out this task.

Postgraduate Studies

Chapter 7

Postgraduate Degree Courses

In explaining the structure of postgraduate degrees in this chapter, we are using the Australian university for our model. What we describe will apply in general terms to postgraduate degree courses in other institutions and in other countries. There are, however, also some important differences. For more detailed information about Australian institutions, see the references listed at the end of this chapter. For variations that apply in Britain, Canada and the United States, consult Appendices 1–3.

We are concerned here only with advanced courses offered at universities and colleges. The range of short training programmes and other award courses is too varied to be covered in this general survey. For detailed information about professional and postgraduate programmes overseas, consult some of the handbooks listed in Appendices 1–3 and also write to the relevant Embassy or High Commission in your own country.

In Australia, as in Asian countries, only a small proportion of students who complete their undergraduate degrees continue to any form of postgraduate training. Those who do decide to continue usually do so for one of two reasons: either they wish to get a professional qualification, such as a Graduate Diploma in Teaching English as a Foreign Language, in Librarianship or in Forestry Management or else they want to do more advanced studies or research in their field, working towards a Master's or PhD degree. It is also common for postgraduate students to move from the institution where they completed their undergraduate studies because their interests have become more specialized. They now enrol in another university, in a college or a technical institute where a particular course or group of specialists can be found — they may even, like you, go abroad to a foreign university.

Degree structures

When you start your postgraduate course, you will find that it is viewed as a **continuation** and extension of undergraduate training rather than as a wholly new beginning. Therefore your lecturers and supervisors will expect you to have completed an undergraduate training similar to that described in the previous four chapters. You will be expected to be competent in the academic skills and study habits we have outlined there. If you are enrolling in a Graduate Diploma or a Master's degree by **coursework**, then the explanations of teaching and learning styles which we have given in those chapters will be relevant to the ways in which you will be studying, though now you will be working at a more advanced level. If you are enrolling for a research **thesis-based** degree, however, there will be significant shifts in your approach which we will examine in more detail in Chapters 8 and 9.

Let us now look at the various diploma and degree courses available at postgraduate level. First we have set out in a chart the relationship between the various courses, and then we explain each degree programme in greater detail.

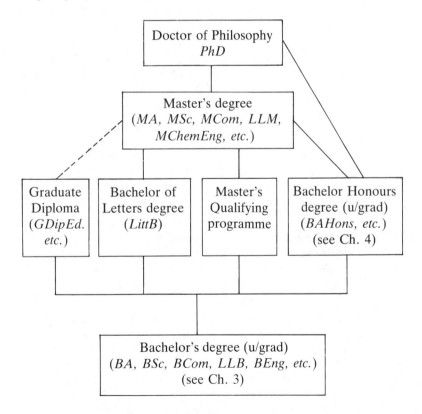

Figure 2: The relation between undergraduate and postgraduate diplomas and degrees

In Australia it is common for students to work their way through the degree levels without a break. Some postgraduates may also work as tutors while completing their PhD. The Asian pattern of teaching or working for some years between each degree level is not so usual in Australia.

1 Graduate Diploma

These diploma courses, which may be offered either in colleges or universities, usually give students who have completed the general Bachelor's degree a more specific vocational training and professional qualification. For example, a BA student may enrol for a Graduate Diploma in Education in order to become a secondary school teacher; a BSc student may take a Graduate Diploma in Food Technology in order to work in the food exporting business; a BEc student may enter a graduate diploma course in Business Management. Most diploma programmes consist of compulsory coursework and may also require a limited project report or sub-thesis. They generally take one year or eighteen months to complete. Most students, when they have been awarded their diploma, seek employment. Some diploma courses are terminal — that is, they do not qualify a student to proceed to a Master's programme — but some can be a qualification for admission to Master's degree studies.

2 Bachelor of Letters (LittB)

This degree is only offered at some universities. It is open to students who wish to continue with postgraduate studies but do not have an Honours degree. The programme, like the Graduate Diploma, most often consists of both coursework and a sub-thesis but it may last for two years. If a student achieves high level results in this course, he is then permitted to continue to an advanced degree. In this way the LittB course can substitute for the Honours year in the Bachelor's degree.

3 Master's Degree (MA, MSc, LLM, etc.) and Master's Qualifying programmes

Graduates who gain a 2A or 1st class Honours degree can apply for admission to a Master's degree programme. In some universities there is also a Master's Qualifying course open to students who completed their Honours degree but not at the level of 2A or above. The Qualifying course usually consists of coursework only and lasts for one year. If this course is completed at a satisfactory level, the student is then permitted to enrol for the regular Master's degree. It is important to note that a Qualifying course does not lead to the award of a degree or diploma. It is, as its title suggests, simply a means by which a student who is inadequately prepared for direct entry to the Master's course may qualify for admission. As we have already seen, certain diploma courses and the LittB degree can provide alternative routes to admission to the Master's degree.

Some Master's programmes, especially those designed specifically to meet the manpower needs of overseas countries and enrolling only overseas students, may have a preliminary diploma course which serves as a Qualifying programme. For example, the admission requirement for a Master's degree in Agriculture (MAg) at one Australian university are set out as follows:

> Applicants should hold a Bachelor's degree in Agricultural or Biological Science from a college or university. Students are normally enrolled initially for the Diploma in Tropical Agronomy and assessed at the end of Second Term (August). If progress in coursework has been at a satisfactory level, the student is transferred to the Master of Agriculture degree with no check in progress, since coursework is the same for the Diploma and the Master's degree.

The form of study for the Master's degree varies with departments: in some cases it is by coursework, in some it is by thesis only, and in some it involves a combination of these. The degree normally takes two years to complete.

4 Doctor of Philosophy

Entry to a PhD course is normally restricted to those who have completed a Master's degree or have gained a high level of distinction in their Honours year. Once again, practice varies among Faculties: in Arts Faculties Honours graduates usually proceed to a Master's degree before they tackle the PhD, whereas in Science Faculties the best Honours students more commonly continue directly to the PhD. Overseas students, if they lack specific research skills or background knowledge, may be required to complete a Master's course before being considered eligible for PhD studies.

The PhD in Australia is a research degree and is only offered at universities. Doctoral students are expected to work independently, with minimal oversight by a supervisor, on their own research projects or topics and must finally present their findings in a substantial thesis. The thesis should be of a quality worthy of publication in an international journal of the discipline. It must be written in English. Most students take at least three years to complete their PhD and many take considerably longer if, for example, their research involves extended fieldwork or experimentation. The final thesis is usually examined by two or more examiners from other universities, and the student may also be required to explain and defend his research in an oral examination conducted by these examiners.

Conclusion

In postgraduate work you are moving gradually away from the undergraduate situation of being taught by someone else to becoming your own teacher. Every postgraduate who is writing a thesis or undertaking research is assigned to a supervisor (or a group of supervisors). Nevertheless, by the time you are a doctoral student, you may be working in an entirely new area of research in which you are, in a sense, 'more expert' than your supervisor. At this point your supervisor can only offer you general guidance and you must assume independent responsibility for the progress and findings of your own research.

In the next two chapters we shall look in more detail at the role of the supervisor in relation to the graduate student, and then at the strategies which many graduates use while working their way through their Master's and PhD programmes.

Summary

In this chapter we have summarized information about the structure of post graduate degree courses in Australia, including Graduate Diplomas, Master's and PhD degrees. (Information on postgraduate studies in Britain, Canada and the United States is given in Appendices 1–3.)

REFERENCES

Commonwealth Universities Yearbook, Association of Commonwealth Universities, London

Scholarships Guide for Commonwealth Postgraduate Students, Association of Commonwealth Universities, London

T.N. Lockyer (ed), *Postgraduate Training in Australia* (Handbook for Overseas Students), Australian Universities' International Development Program/AVCC, Canberra, 1982

MORE TO THINK ABOUT

1 Draw up a diagram of advanced degree courses offered at universities and colleges in your country.

Compare this system with that of Australia, as outlined in this chapter, or of the country in which you plan to study. (When you go abroad you will find it useful to be able to explain, clearly, the similarities and differences between the two degree systems.)

2 If possible, glance through a Master's or PhD thesis written by a colleague or fellow student while studying at an overseas university or college. Then compare what you find with a thesis written in your own Department.

Discuss with a fellow student any differences you notice in:
  ● length,
  ● structure,
  ● the kind of data used and the manner of presentation,
  ● style, and
  ● format.

3 Try to arrange a discussion among colleagues who have already undertaken postgraduate studies overseas. Questions that you might raise include:
  ● what problems did your colleagues meet in adapting to the system of postgraduate studies in a foreign setting?
  ● how did they find the amount and level of academic work compared with their previous experience at home?
  ● how would they explain the advantages and disadvantages of coursework degrees and thesis degrees?
  ● how far have their experiences in studying for their postgraduate qualification overseas been relevant to their teaching and research on return to your country?

(If it is difficult to arrange such a discussion, you may at least be able to interview your teacher of English or some foreign academic staff to discuss their experiences of study abroad in contrast to study within your own country.)

Chapter 8
What Supervisors Expect of Postgraduates

As a postgraduate student you will be assigned to a supervisor, usually a member of the department in which you are registered. Depending on the university you attend and your area of research, you may find that a supervisory committee, rather than a single academic, is appointed but in such cases you will still have one member of the group assigned as your main supervisor.

The relationship between the research student and the supervisor is, obviously, extremely important. It can become the source of many problems if there are misunderstandings or unclear expectations on either side. While it is usually possible for you to change supervisors if a breakdown in the relationship occurs, such a step is unusual and may cause difficulty both for yourself and the department — and may also delay the progress of your research. It is, therefore, important that you understand clearly what supervisors expect of their research students, and what you can expect from your supervisor. This should help you to avoid some of the more obvious pitfalls.

We begin this chapter with an account of the general expectations of supervisors and then discuss some of the particular problems that can arise for overseas students in meeting these expectations.

General expectations

Most supervisors hold certain general expectations about the capacities and previous training of their research students. They assume that these students are:

- very competent in their academic work,
- capable of handling theory and concepts at an advanced level,
- willing to acquire new research skills and techniques, and
- motivated to work independently.

Let us now look in more detail at what is expected of you as a postgraduate student.

1 Initial competencies

If you are starting on a Master's programme, your supervisor will
expect, almost without thinking, that you have behind you all the
skills and experience of four years undergraduate training, as
outlined in the previous chapters. If you are starting a doctoral programme, he will expect you to have either an outstanding undergraduate record (for example, some students, especially in Science,
are permitted to proceed directly from a good Honours degree to a
PhD programme) or else a substantial Master's degree programme
from which you can now develop more advanced research skills.

More specifically, your supervisor will expect you to be competent in:

a the **discipline** in which you plan to do research, including
  • familiarity with the main concepts and theories,
  • experience in appropriate research methodology, and
  • proficiency in the language and techniques through which
    the discipline is developed.

b elementary **research strategies**, including
  • the use of library resources and search systems,
  • the use, where appropriate, of laboratory facilities and tech-
    nical equipment,
  • the capacity to present and participate in departmental semi-
    nars, and
  • some experience in the collection, processing and analysing
    of data.

c **writing strategies** which are appropriate to the production of a
  thesis and, in the case of doctoral candidates, of articles or
  papers at a standard worthy of international publication **in English**.

2 Acquisition of new skills

Your supervisor will expect that you are capable of acquiring any
additional skills or knowledge you require for your research. Like
many other students, you may, for example, find it necessary to
learn how to use a computer system, either for the first time or one
which is different from that which you know already. It may be useful to learn to use a word processor, so that the writing up and editing of articles and your thesis is made less time-consuming. If you
are doing research in Science or Engineering, there are likely to be
new techniques and new technologies which you must master if you

are to take full advantage of the facilities available at your institution.

Additional work may sometimes be necessary to fill in a gap in previous training. Your supervisor, for example, may recommend that you take a course in theory or in research methodology or in basic statistics. In a Master's degree by coursework this training can often be fitted into the overall programme. It is less common for a doctoral student in Australia to undertake coursework, but it can be arranged when necessary.

In general, however, it remains your responsibility to gain the skills necessary for your research; your supervisor will offer suggestions and guidance only.

3 Capacity to work independently

Your supervisor expects that you will be capable of working with increasing independence over the span of your degree. If you are a Master's student, your programme may involve some formal coursework but you will also be required to produce a substantial thesis, based either on data you have collected or on secondary sources. If you are a PhD candidate, your thesis will be the result of an even more extended piece of independent research, involving fieldwork or extensive experiments or a detailed study of sources. Your research should 'contribute to knowledge in the field' and be an independent and individual contribution to learning.

The capacity to study independently for an advanced degree demands a multitude of personal qualities — in particular, motivation and self-confidence — apart from the more specific skills of selecting a promising research topic, developing appropriate research designs and techniques, and finally writing your thesis. Your supervisor's role in this process is to advise, guide and criticize constructively; his aim is always to encourage you towards greater independence in your thinking and your judgement. This attitude, which is common among supervisors in Australian universities, may contrast with the tradition of greater involvement of supervisors with their students in some American and British universities. There are, of course, variations between supervisors. The differences depend partly on individual character and the relationship between student and supervisor, partly on the number of students assigned to the supervisor, partly on the traditional attitudes to supervision within the department, and partly on the level of the supervisor's interest in the student's area of research. Here is the way one supervisor in a Science department described his responsibilities towards his research students:

In the early stages a student needs to be led along and guided in his reading and early experimental work. But if he/she develops as a good scholar the supervisor should gradually retreat to the position of devil's advocate (critic), providing stimulus and criticism, but not imposing on the student's academic abilities any undue influence. But once again the weak student whose work is not going well cannot be treated in this way if the thesis is to be acceptable. Here the supervisor must intervene in a more positive way and **guide** in a more positive way.

More extensive discussion of this subject — the kinds of assistance which research students can normally expect from their supervisors — is offered in Chapter 9.

Particular problems for overseas students

Experienced supervisors recognize that overseas students are likely to have additional difficulties in adjusting to the demands of a research degree. Their problems commonly fall into the following categories:

- relations with their supervisor,
- selection of the research topic,
- participation in discussions, and
- writing the thesis in English.

Whereas all research students will run into difficulties in some of these areas, overseas students may experience more initial confusion and more serious long-term problems.

1 Relations with supervisor

Like many overseas students you may find it difficult to establish a mutually satisfactory relationship with your supervisor. At first you may find the differences in social behaviour confusing. For example, you may worry about how you should address your supervisor: how formal or informal should you be? This problem is usually solved by the supervisor himself; he sets the pattern by the way he addresses you. Otherwise you can often find out the correct approach from other students in the department. In general there is much less formality in speech within Australian universities than in many Asian institutions. First names are commonly used and there is much outward 'equality'.

Supervisors themselves recognize the difficulties that can follow from this cultural difference in social behaviour. One professor described it in these terms:

The relationship between a supervisor and a Master's or PhD student is a personal one and unless a good rapport develops between the two, the student's life will be unhappy . . . The politeness of foreign students is, no doubt, related to their cultural backgrounds. The deference shown to lecturers creates a gap which is hard to cross in terms of scientific communication. When a student is lost in a discussion, he might be too scared to ask a lecturer for an explanation. A supervisor may have great difficulty in finding out what a student wants to do. Initially, at any rate, foreign students are reluctant to show initiative and they strive to do what they think their supervisor wants them to do.

This difference can be a source of further confusion. For example, the relationship between a senior staff member and a promising postgraduate student in an Asian university may be very close: a father/son relationship, or a teacher/pupil, or even a patron/client. In western countries this attitude would not be common; a supervisor would regard it as an invasion of his privacy if his student **expected** him to take a deep interest in his personal welfare. Equally it is not customary for a postgraduate student to give presents to his supervisor. The relationship is strictly academic, but it is expected that the student will eventually reach the status of a colleague of his present supervisor.

2 Selection of the research topic

The problems associated with selecting and developing a research topic affect all students. There is nearly always a period of uncomfortable uncertainty while the student and supervisor together clarify and negotiate a viable project. Overseas students may, in addition, be hampered by differences in their background training and by directions from their home government or university. They may be required to do research on a specific topic which will be of value to their country's administration or national research programme. In some cases, too, the data relevant for a particular project may be inadequate or unavailable. Listen to a supervisor in Applied Sciences explain the different constraints on Australian and foreign students starting on a research programme:

The Australian student seeking entry to a research programme has usually undertaken a 4-year degree within the discipline of proposed research, and hopefully, at least is in a position of familiarity with the state of the art in his discipline, the research organizations and individuals of reputation in the field, and the means whereby consultation and advice on research options may be found.

In contrast, the choice of a research topic and association with the research supervisor can be the first major academic problem that requires solution for the overseas student.

It is rare, in my experience, that an overseas student has a well-defined research programme in mind, despite the confident outlines that can be found in many files or nomination papers. It is the rare student who would not be perfectly happy to join an Australian research team in efforts directed to the problems of Australian society so long as this would lead to the PhD degree in the minimum time, an understandable response in view of the status this would provide on return home. The more difficult problem of defining a research programme that satisfied Australian academic requirements and at the same time has a high relevance to the development needs and problems of the home country, is one of the first obstacles to be overcome.

On the surface it might appear that some overseas students enjoy an advantage over Australian research students. Many Asian students will have had an opportunity to participate in research projects even before undertaking postgraduate studies abroad. Yet this experience may not always be as useful as it seems: the nature of the research is often very different, and the student trainee is usually given a very limited assignment within the programme. A supervisor experienced in developing Asian research programmes has commented on this situation:

Commonly, the mode of their [research trainees'] participation in a research project, which was often government-commissioned, was partial, fragmented, mechanical, marginal, and subordinate. Moreover there were found very few among the trainees who had participated in a research project throughout its entire course of activities, i.e. from the very beginning stage of conceptualization of a research problem to the very end stage of report writing. Again, very few of them had been given the opportunity to understand the overall purpose of the research project, let alone the task of formulating a design for it. Most of them had been temporarily employed by the funding agency or assigned by their superior to join the project as a research assistant playing the role of an interviewer, coder, enumerator, tabulator, or partial report writer. That kind of research experience had made no significant contribution to improving the trainee's research capability.

Yet, as the supervisor knows, it is precisely this capacity for independent management of a research project that is necessary for successful postgraduate studies.

And the first step in that project is getting down to the business of defining a research proposal. This may take some time; refining and narrowing a general interest in an area down to a feasible research proposal. Your supervisor will help you in this process. He can make you aware of the advantages and disadvantages of different lines of research. He will ensure that what you propose is manageable and that it lies within the resources of the department. But he will expect the initiative to come from you.

3 Participation in discussions

The third area of advanced study which presents particular problems for Asian students is participation in academic discussion. Even in discussions between the supervisor and his student there can be problems of communication. One supervisor has described this difficulty as follows:

> My colleagues and I find overseas students to be far more dependent [than local students] on their supervisors for guidance and support. In part this is related to the handicaps noted earlier (language, lack of facilities in home universities, etc.) but is perhaps more associated with the cultural differences between overseas and Australian students. The culture of most ASEAN countries requires a polite deference to and agreement with seniority, whether deserved or not, and this can be a problem in debating research issues.

So this problem is, in part, linguistic. When you are in a discussion with your supervisor or at a seminar, you will find that everyone else seems to speak English fluently and can find the right word or phrase with ease. They also talk fast, colloquially and confidently — and often with a puzzling English accent. But the problem is also in part cultural, as it raises the whole question of attitudes of politeness and respect. Your supervisor is keen that you should ask questions, criticize the ideas of others, and risk trying out new ideas and alternative interpretations in discussion with colleagues. Here is another academic expressing his view on the importance of critical discussion:

> There is still, in 1980, too much evidence among Asian students in particular that training is based on lecture courses without adequate supporting analytical or critical study. Even more fundamental, the student often has no academic tradition of criticizing facts as they are presented verbally or in print . . . The foreign student is often reluctant at first to enter into debate with his fellows or with staff members but I like to think that the experience of hearing a lowly Master's degree student disagree with the professor at a seminar will help to encourage freedom of thought and expression.

This emphasis on participation in seminar discussion is part of an academic tradition that collaboration and criticism are important strategies for learning. Seminars are useful training grounds for postgraduates. Here you can gain competence and confidence in your research. At some stage in your programme you will be required to present a formal paper on the progress and findings of your research, and to lead the discussion which follows. This is one valuable way of getting advice and criticism from a wider group than just yourself and your supervisor. Most students, whether foreign or Australian, dread this experience in advance. Yet, later, students regard their first seminar presentation as an important step in gaining confidence in the quality of their research.

4 Writing the thesis

Although this is usually the final stage of the research programme, it is the stage at which many supervisors and overseas students experience the greatest frustration. It is extremely difficult to produce original ideas of a high quality in your own language; it is much more difficult to attempt this in a foreign language. You may feel trapped by your lack of fluency in the written forms of English. Yet any overseas student who assumes that 'the professor can correct the English in my thesis after I have written it' has a false understanding of the role of supervisor. Few supervisors are prepared to spend time improving the inadequate style and expression of research students. In some universities there may be special facilities or tutors who can offer this assistance. If this help is not available, however, you will be expected to cope with this problem yourself.

So a supervisor in an Australian university has many unexpressed expectations about the competence of his graduate students. You may, because of cultural difference, different mother tongue and different education, have particular problems in meeting these expectations and you may find little assistance is available. But don't despair. In the next chapter we outline some of the strategies other postgraduates have found useful in coping with these problems.

Summary

In this chapter we have examined the assumptions a supervisor holds about the abilities of his research students and the particular problems he expects may arise with overseas students. In general the supervisor expects his postgraduate students to be competent in their discipline, to be ready to acquire new research skills, and to be capable of working independently on their research project.

Overseas students may find that they have particular problems, caused partly by linguistic and partly by cultural differences, in
- relations with their supervisor,
- selection of the research topic,
- participation in discussions, and
- writing their thesis in English.

MORE TO THINK ABOUT

1 If you have any experience in a research project already, analyse the part you played in it. (If you have not had such experience, interview another student who has.)

In the course of your analysis (or interview), make notes in answer to the following questions:
- what stages of the project were you involved in?
- what part did you play in each of these stages?
- to what extent did you feel you understood and participated in the overall management of the project? (Compare your answer with the comment quoted on p. 94.)

On the basis of your notes and what we have said in this chapter about independent research, write further notes identifying the areas in which you may need to develop new skills and confidence.

2 Some of the senior academic staff in your department may have acted as supervisors. Find out from one of these staff what expectations he holds about his research students.

You might base your questions on the issues we have raised in this chapter. For example:
- what **initial competencies** would the supervisor assume that his research students have in:
  — the discipline?
  — research strategies?
  — writing skills?
- what **new skills** would a student be expected to learn in order to undertake a research programme or degree in your department?
- how important is the ability to work **independently?**
- how important is the student's **participation** in seminars and other discussions?

Make notes about your findings and discuss them with two or three classmates. In particular, what differences can you identify between the expectations of supervisors in your own department and those we have outlined for supervisors in departments abroad?

3 Go to a seminar or discussion in your department (or in your university or college) and analyse what happens there. Notice:
  - how many people participate in the discussion,
  - whether there are some people who do not speak at all,
  - who talks most,
  - whether the seminar leader deliberately tries to get people to participate, and how he or she does this,
  - how people signal to the seminar leader that they wish to speak, and
  - whether people contradict or criticize each other's ideas.

After the other members of your class have also had a chance to observe a seminar in this way, discuss your findings together.

What do you think may be the main problems for you participating in seminars when you go abroad? Can you think of any strategies which might help you overcome these problems?

Chapter 9
Strategies for Postgraduate Studies

'Postgraduate research is basically a lonely activity' — this is how one postgraduate summed up her experience of studying for her PhD degree. At the start of your degree programme you may feel daunted by the prospect of so many years of problems and effort stretching ahead of you. Yet you can take heart; the majority of postgraduate students **do** gain their degrees, and there are various strategies for coping with the difficulties likely to arise at each stage of your research programme. In this chapter we shall look at some of the more common strategies so that you can adapt them to suit your own style of working.

In the last chapter we saw postgraduate students' problems from the viewpoint of the supervisor. Now we are looking at the same problems from a student's perspective. Here we shall concentrate on those four areas identified in the previous chapter as likely to provide most difficulties: relations with your supervisor; choosing and developing your research topic; taking part in formal and informal discussions of academic matters; and planning, writing and presenting your thesis.

1 Relations with supervisor

Nearly all research students, whether local or from overseas, experience difficulties with their supervisors at some stage of their course. Sometimes these difficulties arise from a difference of personality or expectations. One student complains that his supervisor demands too much contact; he schedules weekly meetings and requires weekly progress reports in writing. Another student feels her supervisor has abandoned her; he is never available in his office, is frequently overseas on his own research projects, and has only spoken twice to her in the whole year. Your own experience is likely to fall somewhere between these two extremes.

Of course the students themselves may contribute to these difficulties. Some students often feel shy about approaching their supervisors; others feel uncomfortable if they disagree with some criticism or advice given by a supervisor; many think their supervisors are 'too busy' to spend time working with them on a problem that has arisen in their research or writing. And some overseas students expect their supervisors to guide them closely at every point of their research and to edit their thesis for them on all points of style and grammatical accuracy.

Another common source of problems stems from the changing nature of the relationship with your supervisor during the different stages of your research programme. The relationship is not static. It typically divides into three stages:

a at first your supervisor is likely to act as a director and instructor. He has all the experience, and you have very little. He is competent in research design, in the use of relevant technology, in techniques; he 'knows the field'. And you are a beginner.

b during the fieldwork or experimental stage, however, your relations will change. Now you are becoming basically competent and may even surpass your supervisor in detailed knowledge of your particular research area. He may act as critic and general guide, but the relationship is nearer to being colleagues in a common endeavour than being master and pupil. Whereas, at the beginning, your supervisor set a regular time for you to meet him so that he could check on your progress, now he is likely to take a less active role. You may meet in a lab, but as members of a research team; you may meet in departmental seminars, but as colleagues.

c however, when you move on to the final stage — writing the thesis — your relationship is likely to change again. Because of his greater experience your supervisor will probably again take up a dominant role. He becomes both a critical commentator on your actual writing and a disciplinary expert discussing the meaning and implications of your research. Some students find difficulty in shifting back to a subordinate role, and relations with their supervisors can become strained at this stage, especially as the period of writing up is often a time of particular tension and pressure. More will be said about this in the section on writing a thesis.

For the moment, the main point to grasp is that your supervisor is an **adviser**. He advises from his vantage point of superior knowledge and experience, but you are not compelled to follow his advice. His ultimate purpose is to help you grow in the exercise of your independent judgement.

There are, according to experienced postgraduate students, some useful strategies for developing an effective working relationship with a supervisor:

a keep in contact with your supervisor: agree on a schedule of regular meetings (particularly in the early stages of research), hand in summaries of work in progress, inform him of any major changes of plan or direction in your research. If you have more than one supervisor, make sure that you all meet from time to time in a joint discussion of progress. This can avoid problems later, ensuring that you do not become a ping-pong ball between two supervisors who find they cannot agree on a vital point of theory or methodology.

b work out a joint understanding with your supervisor, at an early stage in your programme, about his exact duties and areas of responsibility for your progress; and about your responsibilities in relation to him. For example, few supervisors will accept that it is their duty to edit a thesis for grammatical and stylistic weaknesses. If you know that well in advance, you have the opportunity to seek alternative assistance through private tutoring or help from an English language adviser or a fellow student. If your research is in a scientific field, it is also important to reach an agreement about authorship rights in the publication of joint papers.

c request an official change of supervisor, through the Head of your Department, if your original supervisor is unsuitable; for example, if he is not an expert in the specific topic you finally settle upon, or because you and he clash in personality. Most universities have a system for changing supervisors if there are genuine reasons for the request.

d accept the view that the relationship between you and your supervisor is a 'business' arrangement and that it need not extend to informal and personal contacts — though individual supervisors and students may develop such a relationship.

Above all, be clear about what help you can reasonably expect from your supervisor. You can certainly expect that your supervisor will

- help you select and frame a research topic, and assist you in getting the research under way,
- ensure that you have adequate resources to carry out your research, and

- advise you both on the content of your thesis and papers and on their format and style of presentation as well.

Beyond this, the amount of further assistance you receive is a matter for negotiation between you and your supervisor. Because he regards you as capable of independent study, your supervisor will normally expect you to take the initiative in asking for help. As a postgraduate student, you are expected to take the primary responsibility for your own progress.

2 Selecting and developing the research topic

Selecting a research topic is not something you can expect to do immediately. It usually takes time and considerable discussion. You may have come to Australia with a clear idea of the area in which you plan to do research — or maybe your government or university has sponsored your studies in an area of particular interest to them. But in fact a lot of development and change is likely to occur before your final topic is agreed upon between yourself, your supervisor and the department.

The process of selecting a topic starts as a deliberately tentative set of questions directed to a specific point, whether a period of history, an economic model or a scientific problem. As you proceed with your reading or experimentation, some of the tentative questions fall away, as they are clearly not productive or relevant. Other questions grow in importance, and eventually form the aims or hypotheses which underpin your research.

This early stage of developing a topic can be a period of both excitement and anxiety. Other students who have gone through this period of confusion offer the following advice:

a use your supervisor's greater knowledge and experience to the full. He can direct you towards topics which seem promising, warn you off areas or problems that have already been covered or have proved unfruitful, and discuss with you the implications of your choice.

b complete as much reading — 'literature survey' — as possible in the early stages. In this way you become aware of the whole range of options in your field before you narrow your focus down to a manageable area of research. Make notes as you go, so that a bibliographic record is started from day one of your programme and is built up throughout the course of your study. Apart from deepening your understanding, this saves time later when you have to write a full literature review and draw up a comprehensive bibliography, or list of references, for your thesis.

c do not rely only on your supervisor and your own reading. Use the other resources available in the university. Other academics in the department, fellow students, other universities and colleges in the country, national conferences, departmental seminars and discussions over coffee are all potentially valuable sources of ideas. They also provide opportunities for refining, through discussion and debate, your own understanding of your topic and research.

d welcome rather than shrink away from, opportunities to try out your developing ideas on staff and fellow students. It can be very useful — though frightening — to give a departmental seminar on your proposed research topic early in your course, maybe after six months or a year. This forces you to clarify your objectives and provides you with a chance to get constructive criticism from other members of the department. It also has the benefit of making you known to staff within your department.

e set aside some regular time each week for writing about your research — even if it is only a private record for your own interest. Writing enables you to reflect systematically, to clarify and build up ideas over time. At first this writing may be very rough, uncertain, informal; but it will become more fluent as your understanding grows and as your control of an appropriate style of English improves. Further, these rough notes can later provide the foundation for papers and chapters of your thesis.

All these suggestions point in the same direction: you must allow yourself plenty of time and you must make use of all the resources available when choosing your research topic. You will be devoting a lot of your time and energy to working on your topic, so it is important that it is one that satisfies you.

3 Participating in discussions

As we saw in the previous chapter, tutorials and seminars are regarded by supervisors as valuable opportunities for developing your critical abilities as well as extending your knowledge. Many of the problems overseas students face in public discussions, and the strategies for dealing with them, are common at both the undergraduate and postgraduate levels. Therefore before you read any further, turn back to Chapter 6 and read the section 'Tutorials and laboratory sessions'. The strategies for participating in formal discussions which are described there — writing out and learning some preparatory comments, conducting 'unofficial' tutorials, etc. — may be of assistance to you in postgraduate seminars.

There are two other strategies which postgraduates say they have found useful:

a attend as many seminars as possible in the first year of your degree programme, even seminars outside your own department and special area of interest. These can all add to your experience even if you do not have the confidence to participate at first. You can still learn a lot merely by observing. Notice when and how other participants intervene in order to ask a question: how do they make critical comments? how do they attack and defend arguments? what special phrases do they use to show respect and politeness even when they are voicing disagreement? how do they signal to the seminar leader or chairman that they wish to ask a question or make a point?

b practise in a systematic way some of these oral skills of explanation, questioning, attack and defence. Use some of the special phrases you have heard; try to recall some of the signals people used to attract attention. At first you may only be able to do this in the privacy of your own room, rehearsing what you might have said in answer to a question or point of criticism. It can be useful to write out some questions, or your defence of an argument, and read this aloud, and then try to repeat it without referring to the paper. As you build up confidence and fluency, look for informal situations in which you can test your ideas — with other students, maybe, or with your supervisor. (Here you have a real advantage over undergraduates learning to take part in tutorials: whereas they are beginners in their discipline and have to worry whether their ideas may seem foolish, you are already reasonably expert in your knowledge of your discipline.)

Out of all this informal training will eventually come the confidence to participate in public discussions. That moment marks an important development in your training. Listen to how one supervisor describes this step:

> The first real evidence that we are succeeding with a student is the occasion when, without being prompted, he asks his first question in a seminar. Another great step forward is the first occasion when a student is prepared to criticize, during discussion, the work of other people. After this has happened we become aware that the student is a fully-fledged member of our postgraduate and research community.

It is also important to master the art of asking questions and joining in discussions in a less formal setting than a seminar. In order to make full use of the facilities of the university, you need to ask questions, ask for information, ask for help. Start by asking questions of other students, then of the departmental secretary, then of library staff and lab technicians. Here is the advice of a senior postgraduate to new students on how to find their way around a strange lab:

> In an unfamiliar laboratory finding and knowing where/how to obtain chemicals, glassware, etc. is frequently difficult. Rather than learning things the hard way, i.e. by experience, not knowing where to order things etc., try and find out which person in the lab/dept knows where everything is and if not, how to get it (by hook or by crook!). Then rather than spend fruitless hours searching for stuff, simply go and ask this person (usually a younger technician with a few years experience in the lab; older ones tend, generally, to be less helpful) for advice.

So the main strategies are: **observe**, **practise**, and **participate**. As we have stressed in a number of places, these three strategies provide a sound basis for successful study in a foreign culture — not merely for participating in seminars but for writing papers and theses as well.

4 Writing the thesis

The thesis is the culmination of your whole research programme. It stands as both the public record and the measure of your thinking and your research. It may never be widely read but it must be able to stand up to rigorous academic criticism. Note that here we are only concerned with thesis writing. If you have to write essays and shorter papers as part of your coursework, you should read Chapter 5 and Chapter 6 section 5, and consult the list of references in Appendix 4. These sections and some of the references which we list also deal with the related problems of reading.

The general problems of writing a thesis seem to be clear enough. They include:

- ordering the material in a logical sequence,
- developing a clear prose style,
- maintaining a steady rate of production, often within a tight time schedule, and
- arranging for the final typing, binding and formal presentation of the completed work.

And, through all this, you have to keep up your energy and

motivation. Listen to what a Science student has to say about this last point:

> It can be useful to point out that the nature of thesis work is greatly different to undergraduate work. Most importantly, there are (often) no distinct short-term goals. Such goals can help a student's morale by giving him/her a sense of achievement and a feeling of 'getting somewhere'. They are also helpful in assessing one's progress. Compared with undergraduate years where one has regular goals — distinct steps towards that ultimate goal — in the form of exams and passing a year, a PhD may last 3 or 4 years without any such distinct stages or feelings of achievement. Progress may often be in such small, gradual steps that the student does not have a feeling of overall accomplishment. He does not see what he has done — only what he has left to do.

Of course the problems do vary with individuals and with the nature of the thesis. In scientific and technical research, for example, finding a satisfactory research problem, design and experimental technique is often the really creative act. Writing up the material as a thesis, though important, is more a matter of hard work and self-discipline. The format and organization of scientific theses are well-established. In Arts and Social Science disciplines, however, the writing itself may constitute the creative act; the thesis may embody both the substance and the form of all your research, since there is no external body of data or experimentation which can be pointed to as evidence of your years of work.

While the general problems of thesis writing may be clear enough, the strategies for dealing with them are less obvious. This is partly because writing is so individual, and partly because the structures and styles of theses vary so much between disciplines. Most Biochemistry theses look like other Biochemistry theses, but they are very different from theses in English or Economics or Law. There are, however, some general strategies for thesis writing that do appear to be useful:

a   consult a number of theses which have been written by former postgraduate students in your department (one copy of each successful thesis is normally kept in the departmental library and another in the university library). Though you must be cautious of taking such theses as exact models for your own work, they are useful guides. They will give you, from the outset, some notion of the standard for which you must aim and some familiarity with the more common styles of presentation. Take note too of such details as the average length of these theses and the sections into which they are commonly divided (is there always a literature review? a separate section on results?). Look, too, at the approximate proportions of different sections (how much analysis of theory, for example, and how much description of fieldwork or methods?). Besides their usefulness as guides, these theses can also give you some reassurance. They demonstrate that other students have succeeded in overcoming the same hazards that you now face.

b write frequently. Do not postpone all your writing until the last stage when you have become so out of practice that writing is extremely difficult. You may find you have little choice in this matter. Many supervisors demand regular progress reports; and where they don't, we have already suggested that you provide them anyway. You may be asked to write a literature review at an early stage (which can be revised later for inclusion in your thesis). You may be encouraged to write up parts of your fieldwork or experimentation as you go, or to write papers for joint publication with your supervisor. In our university we have conducted a survey of supervisors about the process of thesis writing. The point most frequently stressed in their comments was that students should 'practise writing' throughout their programme. They suggested writing short summaries, articles, papers, draft chapters, even short stories. We have ourselves earlier recommended keeping a private record of work-in-progress.

c talk about your work to anyone in the department who will listen. Through discussion you can often clarify ideas and gain new insights. Talking can be an important preparatory stage on the path to more systematic structuring of ideas through writing.

Also, discuss with your supervisor and fellow students any problems you are having with writing. Do not try to hide the fact that you find writing in English difficult. Some students avoid showing draft chapters to their supervisor. As one Thai student commented: 'Most overseas students who have overriding problems with English will feel reluctant and ashamed to submit their works to the supervisor.' Yet if you act in this way, you cut off the chance for early assistance. Worse, you can create the possibility that your supervisor may not recognize your weakness until the final writing stage — when it is extremely difficult to do much about it.

d use your strength in your own first language to compensate for any weakness in English. Though your thesis must finally be presented in English, this does not mean that all of your initial thinking and writing must be done in English. Especially at the beginning and especially when you are dealing with concepts and abstractions, it is often easier to write in your first language. You can then translate this, maybe with help from another student in your department who is both English-speaking and understands your materials. Much of the intellectual frustration and feeling of incompetence that overseas students have comes from problems of thinking in a second language. They know the statements they can make in English are so much more simplified and naive than their thinking in their own language.

e find a system for writing that suits your own working habits. There is no single best way to write a thesis. People will offer you dogmatic advice based on their personal experience, as though their methods must work for everyone else. Here is how one Science supervisor advises his students:

> Write the thesis as a **whole**, not chapter by chapter. Shuffle topics to chapters as you write them, but have a full outline from the beginning. Write when all the work has been done, and work for a short period — don't drag it out over a year or two.

> When writing my thesis I worked 5 weeks straight. Then took four weeks vacation, far away from the university. On my return I worked 7 days a week for 4 more weeks, after which the thesis was submitted. Every word was changed in the last four weeks, and the result was a great improvement. The break away from it all allowed me to treat my draft as someone else's and write a fresh version, yet still benefitting from all previous exertions of the mind.

Yet clearly, this 'pressure-cooker' system would not work for all students; and it might be very unsuitable for writing a thesis in the Humanities where ideas often need to be mapped out again and again, to be refined by being written over and over until the concept finds its perfect wording. Seek the advice of others, therefore, but use it critically in the light of your knowledge about how you work best.

On a related matter: try to keep separate in your mind the functions of the first and later drafts of your chapters. The function of the first drafting is to clarify **for yourself** what you think; the act of writing is in itself an act of clarifying. The function of later drafting is to find more effective ways of presenting what you think **to your readers**. Only at this stage do questions of format, correctness, style, and other formal conventions begin to matter. Again a postgraduate student in Science has this sensible comment to make:

> Don't try to make your first draft your final one — it's often more important to get your ideas down on paper in rough form than to become over-concerned with style etc. in the early drafts.

f arrange well in advance for any assistance you may need in editing your thesis. The final polish on your writing (making sure it follows the appropriate conventions of grammar, style and format) may be crucial to the acceptance of the thesis. There is a great deal you can do for yourself with painstaking use of grammars and dictionaries (both general and subject specialist ones) and by close attention to the presentation of other theses that have been passed in your department. You can also enlist the help of fellow students and friends. The university or some sponsoring organizations may provide financial assistance or special tutors for such editing. In some fortunate cases your supervisor may be willing to read and correct the whole thesis for its English and style, but you cannot rely on this. So it is important that you prepare to meet this problem before it actually arises; in the words of the English proverb 'Forewarned is forearmed'.

g allow sufficient time before your submission date for the final typing, proof-reading and binding of the thesis. You are expected to make these arrangements yourself. You will need to find a competent typist, particularly if your thesis involves complex mathematical formulae or intricate tables and diagrams. Most departments can recommend typists who have experience in typing theses, and they can also advise you where to get it bound for final presentation. But this stage does take considerable time, so take this into account when planning the last months of your work.

There is one final step before your thesis is accepted and your degree can be granted. Commonly, at least at the PhD level, you are required to 'defend' your thesis in an oral examination conducted by the academics who have been appointed as your official examiners. During this session the examiners, who will already have read and discussed your thesis among themselves, may raise criticisms, queries and points of misunderstanding. You are given the opportunity to explain your views, defend and elaborate your argument, and display your grasp of the research. Obviously participation in seminars is a useful preparation for this oral exam. It gives you practice in academic argument and it also develops your confidence that your knowledge of your subject is sound.

Summary

In this chapter we have presented some strategies which experienced postgraduates and supervisors have found useful in coping with the problems overseas students commonly have
- in relations with their supervisors,
- in the choice and development of their research topic,
- in participating in seminars and discussions, and
- in writing and presenting their thesis.

We have emphasized, however, that there is no single correct method of working at postgraduate level. The best strategies will be those you develop for yourself. We suggest that one systematic way to develop your own study habits is to follow these stages:
- observe,
- practise, and
- participate.

By following these procedures you can develop confidence and gain the skills you need for successful postgraduate study.

MORE TO THINK ABOUT

1 Go to the library and make up a bibliography of the books and articles that are relevant to your probable research interest. Include materials in your own language as well as in English, if appropriate.

   Discuss your bibliography with a senior staff member in your department and find out what other sources of information he or she can suggest.

2 In Appendix 6 you will find a brief guide for new postgraduates. This guide was prepared by senior postgraduate students in Botany in an Australian university. After reading this guide, make a team of two or three fellow students and together write an equivalent set of notes for research students in your own department. What advice would be most important to give them?

Compare the notes you produce with the Australian guide. What differences do you see? What particular adjustments will you have to make to your present habits of working when you go abroad to study?

3 Invite two or more students who have completed postgraduate study abroad to talk to your class about:
  • their relationships with their supervisors, and
  • the problems of writing a thesis (in English).

(Make sure that your speakers have seen Chapters 8 and 9 of this book before they give their talk. In this way they can focus on the same issues as you have been thinking about.)

Discuss as a group the issues and problems which their speeches raise. Consider also the extent to which the strategies we have suggested in this chapter provide a basis for tackling those problems.

Appendices

Appendix 1

Tertiary studies in Britain

There are three useful reference manuals, regularly updated:

Higher Education in the UK, 1982–84: A handbook for students and their advisers, Longman, London (published for the British Council and the Association of Commonwealth Universities)

Which Degree: The complete guide to first degree courses (ed. A. Segal), Haymarket, London

Graduate Studies 1981/82: The guide to postgraduate study in the UK, CRAC, Cambridge

These and other reference books should be available in most British Embassies and in British Council offices or libraries.

The British tertiary system includes 45 universities and 31 polytechnics — as well as a host of other colleges and training institutes — located throughout the British Isles. Both universities and polytechnics are supported by government funds, though universities are independently run and are the main centres of academic research. Polytechnics are more directly controlled by the government and offer courses and qualifications which are more technical, vocational and professional in orientation.

The **titles** of administrators and other staff in both universities and polytechnics are largely similar to those used in Australia (see Chapter 3, pp. 22–23). There will, however, be minor variations. In some universities there may be Schools in place of Faculties. In others, staff titles may differ: a tutor in some universities holds a relatively low position in the staff hierarchy whereas a Tutor at Oxford merely means an academic attached to a College. He or she may in fact also hold a post of Lecturer or Reader within the wider university.

Admission to tertiary institutions in Britain depends on performance in the national 'A' level exam — or a recognized equivalent level. Some universities may require an additional entrance exam.

For certain degree courses there may be prerequisites and quotas; admission to any course is dependent on the number of places available. Initial application for first degree admissions to universities is made through the Universities Central Council on Admissions (UCCA); for higher degrees application is normally made directly to the institutions. Admission to polytechnics is not centralized and the level of school attainment required is normally lower.

British universities offer the same range of degrees as Australian: Bachelor's, Master's and PhD degrees, as well as a variety of Diplomas. The **undergraduate degree structure** generally consists either of a three-year degree course with a specialization in one or two subjects, leading to an Honours (or Special) degree; or else of a three-year less specialized set of courses, leading to an Ordinary (or General) degree. In Scotland the first degree, which takes four years, is called a Master's degree. Polytechnic courses differ in length, depending on the level of the diploma or degree and whether they are being studied full-time or in conjunction with employment ('sandwich' courses).

Postgraduate degree courses are similar to those found in Australia (see Chapter 7); theses may also be referred to as dissertations.

The **teaching system** makes use of the same structures (lectures, tutorials/ seminars, and laboratory/practical sessions) and **assessment** is carried out by the same means (formal exams, essays and projects, short tests) as in Australia — though in each case the mix or weighting given to different elements may vary widely between institutions.

Finally, in Britain the three-term year is more common than the two-semester system in both universities and polytechnics, and the academic year normally runs from September to July.

Appendix 2

Tertiary studies in the United States of America

Here are some useful reference manuals, which are regularly up-dated:

> *The College Handbook* (ed. D. Dillenbeck & S. Wetzel), College Entrance Examination Board, New York
> *Guide to American Graduate Schools* (ed. H. Livesey & H. Doughty), Penguin, New York
> *Graduate Programs and Admissions Manuals,* produced by the Graduate Record Examinations Board and the Council of Graduate Schools in the United States
> *Costs at U.S. Educational Institutions*, Institute of International Education, New York
> *The College Blue Book*, 2 vols, Macmillan, New York

A helpful brief guide is *Students' Guide to Study in the USA* by Gene R. Hawes (Macmillan, New York, 1971). The *Handbook on U.S. Study for Foreign Nationals*, produced by the Institute of International Education in New York, is also useful even though it has not been revised since 1973. These and other reference books should be available at most United States Embassies and United States Information Service (USIS) libraries. Some libraries also have videotaped programmes specially for students planning to study in America.

There is a vast network of tertiary institutions in the United States, including two-year Junior or Community Colleges, four-year Colleges offering only first degrees, and Universities and Institutes which offer both first and higher degrees. Some colleges are funded by government; others are funded privately. The quality of institutions varies enormously from the prestigious 'Ivy League' universities such as Harvard and Yale to community-based junior colleges offering courses which are little above the level of secondary school.

The **title** 'faculty' is used in American universities both for individual academic staff and for the staff as a group (compare the usage in Australia, Chapter 3). At the lowest teaching level are graduate assistants and teaching fellows, usually postgraduate students who are combining research with some teaching, and instructors, who are normally on temporary short-term appointments. Most regular faculty start as assistant professors and then move to the rank of associate professor and, finally, professor — despite these distinctions in rank, faculty in all three categories can be addressed as Professor. The head of a university is usually called a President and most of the administrative work is carried out by Deans and their subordinates.

Admission to first-degree studies is usually on the basis of school performance and, for overseas students, proficiency in English. Some colleges may require prospective students to take the widely recognized College Board Scholastic Aptitude Test, or their own admission test. At postgraduate level, apart from performance in the first degree, applicants usually have to take some version of the Graduate Record Examination (GRE) or the Miller Analogies Test (MAT). In the more prestigious universities, admission is highly competitive. In all cases application for admission is made direct to the university or college.

The **undergraduate degree** consists most commonly of a four-year course, with students in each successive year called freshmen, sophomores, juniors and seniors. The first degree is usually a 'liberal arts' degree and includes courses in both Arts and Sciences. More professional and vocational studies are pursued in a subsequent degree course; for example, students only undertake Law or Medicine after they have completed a first degree. The degree is constructed on a credit system in which courses are rated a certain number of credit points on the basis of contact hours and other criteria. A full degree is normally composed of 120 credits, that is 15 credits a semester for a total of eight semesters. Fifteen credits would correspond to four or five courses. Within this total, some courses may be compulsory as part of a major and others are electives, that is, open to choice. In many universities and colleges it is possible for students to take courses for credit during the summer session and so complete their degree in less than four years.

Postgraduate degree courses vary in their structure from total coursework degrees to degrees solely by thesis. However there is often a larger component of coursework, including exams, than in Australian or British postgraduate programmes. The degrees offered are similar to those offered in Australia (see Chapter 7).

The **teaching system** makes use of the same structures (lectures, tutorials/seminars, and laboratory/practical sessions). Lecture classes, however, may be very large. Where such classes are divided into smaller groups, they are often directed by graduate assistants rather than course lecturers or regular academic staff. Much use is made of programmed learning and of technological aids such as computers, language laboratories and audio-visual facilities.

Assessment is usually continuous, in that all assigments and tests contribute to the final grade point score. Multiple-choice exams and written exams are normally also part of the assessment scheme and at graduate level oral exams are frequently used. The following table sets out the standard grading system:

A — excellent — 4
B — above average — 3
C — average — 2
D — pass, but below average — 1
E or F — fail — 0

These grades are used to calculate the student's 'grade point average' which is the most commonly used score of achievement. In most graduate programmes a student would be expected to maintain A or B level grades for all courses.

Finally, in the United States the academic year is divided into two semesters and runs from October to June. Many institutions, however, run a summer session during the long vacation and offer courses which can count towards the degree.

Appendix 3

Tertiary studies in Canada

There are a number of useful references published by universities and government agencies:

Directory of Canadian Universities, Association of Universities and Colleges of Canada, Ottawa

AUCC Information: annual publication of Course Sheets

The College Blue Book, 2 vols, Macmillan, New York

University Study in Canada, (Ref. no. 36), Dept of External Affairs, Ottawa

Canadian Universities and Degree-granting Colleges, (Ref. no. 44), Dept of External Affairs, Ottawa

Information Canada: Information for foreign students on post-secondary study in Canada, Canadian Bureau for International Education, Ottawa

Guide to Foreign Student Authorisations for Canada, Canadian Bureau for International Education, Ottawa

Studying in Canada: facts for Foreign Students, Employment and Immigration Commission, Ottawa

These directories and pamphlets should be available at most Canadian Embassies.

Higher education in Canada, which blends elements of both the British and American systems, is organized on a provincial basis and funded by both the federal and provincial governments (approximately 85%) and by tuition fees (the remaining 15%). There are 65 degree-granting institutions, six of which use French as the medium of instruction.

The **titles** of academic staff generally follow the American pattern: teaching staff are referred to as 'faculty' and the same ranks of assistant professor, associate professor and professor apply and all faculty members can be addressed as Professor. Besides these regular faculty, there are a number of one-year appointees at the rank of 'lecturer' (equivalent to 'instructor' in the American system). The head of a university goes by a variety of titles: Principal, Rector, President, or Vice-Chancellor.

Admission to first-degree studies is normally on the basis of performance in secondary school. For foreign students, some tests or equivalent proof of competence in English is usually required (the TOEFL test is the most common). Entry to Master's and PhD programmes is dependent on performance in first-degree studies — an Honours rather than a General or Ordinary degree is normally required. Some universities also insist that postgraduate applicants take the Graduate Record Examination (GRE). In all cases application for admission is made direct to the university or college.

The **undergraduate degree** consists of a three- to five-year programme of study, successful completion of which is the normal condition for entry to professional and vocational studies. For most Bachelor's degrees in Arts and Sciences, students are required to obtain 90 credits over a three-year programme or 120 credits over four years (depending on the number of years of secondary school and college education). Most students take five courses a semester, each involving a minimum of three hours class time per week.

At the **postgraduate level** some Master's degree programmes, especially in the professional schools, do not require a thesis; others do. For the PhD, however, both coursework and a thesis (or the equivalent) are required.

The **teaching system** makes use of the same structure (lectures, tutorials/seminars, and laboratory/practical sessions) and **assessment** is by a mixture of assignments, tests and formal exams, with the weight given to each of these forms of evaluation varying widely among institutions. Both numerical (percentage) and letter grades are used in a pattern similar to that described for US universities, and these grades may be used to calculate a student's grade point average.

Finally, in Canada the academic year runs from September to June and is divided into two semesters. Many institutions, however, run a summer session during the long vacation and offer courses which can count towards the degree.

Appendix 4

Useful references

Notes: 1 In choosing further reference books, look particularly at the place of publication. Styles of writing and usage can vary significantly between countries, particularly between the US and the UK.
2 Those books marked with an *asterisk are published with the aid of the English Language Book Society (ELBS) and are much cheaper in your own country than abroad. So buy those you want before you leave home.

General reference works

Concise Oxford Dictionary (Clarendon Press, Oxford, 1976) is the standard choice for a portable dictionary for students in the UK and Australia. For more intensive dictionary work, the two-volume *Shorter Oxford English Dictionary* would be preferable. The corresponding authorities for North American students would be *Webster's New Collegiate Dictionary*, and *Webster's Third New International Dictionary* (G. & C. Merriam, Springfield, Mass.). For students whose first language is not English, the most comprehensive and clearly presented dictionary is *A.S. Hornby's Oxford Advanced Learner's Dictionary of Current English* (Oxford University Press, Oxford, 1974).

Roget's Thesaurus (Penguin, London, 1970) is useful for helping you find the exact word.

The *M.H.R.A. Style Book*, 2nd edn (Modern Humanities Research Association, London, 1978) is frequently used in Britain by authors, editors and writers of dissertations.

MLA Handbook (Modern Language Association of America, New York, 1980) is a standard reference manual for American and British academic writing.

Oxford Dictionary for Writers and Editors (Clarendon Press, Oxford, 1981) is a comprehensive guide to spelling of unusual words.

Writing Essays, Papers and Theses

R. Barrass, *Scientists Must Write*, Chapman and Hall, London, 1978
J. Clanchy and B. Ballard, *Essay Writing for Students*, Longman Cheshire, Melbourne, 1981
――――*How To Write Essays*, International edn, Longman Cheshire, Melbourne, 1983
M. O'Connor and F.P. Woodford, *Writing Scientific Papers in English*, Elsevier, Amsterdam, 1975
K.L. Turabian, *Student's Guide for Writing College Papers*, 3 edn, Uni. of Chicago Press, Chicago, 1976

Grammar

*J.B. Heaton and J.P. Stocks, *Overseas Students' Companion to English Studies*, Longman, London, 1966
*A.S. Hornby, *Guide to Patterns and Usage in English*, 2nd edn, Oxford University Press, Oxford, 1975
*R. Quirk and S. Greenbaum, *University Grammar of English*, Longman, London, 1973
*A.J. Thomson and A.V. Martinet, *A Practical English Grammar*, 3 edn, Oxford University Press, Oxford, 1980

Style and Usage

H.W. Fowler, *A Dictionary of Modern English Usage*, 2nd edn rev. by Sir E. Gowers, Clarendon Press, Oxford, 1965
Sir E. Gowers, *The Complete Plain Words*, Penguin, London, 1962
M. Nicholson, *A Dictionary of American-English Usage*, Oxford University Press, New York, 1957
E. Partridge, *Usage and Abusage*, Penguin, London, 1963
――――*You Have a Point There*, Hamish Hamilton, London, 1964
W. Strunk and E.B. White, *Elements of Style*, 3rd edn, Macmillan, New York, 1979
G.A. Wilkes, *A Dictionary of Australian Colloquialisms*, Fontana, Sydney, 1978

Study methods

C. Allen, *Passing Examinations*, rev. edn, Pan Books, London, 1966
C. Parsons, *How to Study Effectively*, Arrow Books, London, 1976
F.P. Robinson, *Effective Study*, Harper and Row, New York, 1970

Appendix 5

Science text (for Chapter 5, exercise 3)

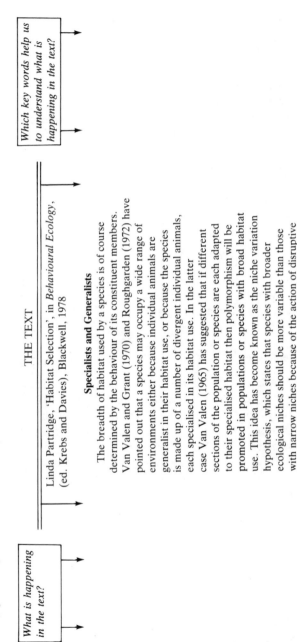

THE TEXT

Linda Partridge, 'Habitat Selection', in *Behavioural Ecology*, (ed. Krebs and Davies), Blackwell, 1978

Specialists and Generalists

The breadth of habitat used by a species is of course determined by the behaviour of its constituent members. Van Valen and Grant (1970) and Roughgarden (1972) have pointed out that a species may occupy a wide range of environments either because individual animals are generalist in their habitat use, or because the species is made up of a number of divergent individual animals, each specialised in its habitat use. In the latter case Van Valen (1965) has suggested that if different sections of the population or species are each adapted to their specialised habitat then polymorphism will be promoted in populations or species with broad habitat use. This idea has become known as the niche variation hypothesis, which states that species with broader ecological niches should be more variable than those with narrow niches because of the action of disruptive selection. Some studies support this contention (Rothstein 1973, Grant *et al.* 1976) while others

What is happening in the text?

Which key words help us to understand what is happening in the text?

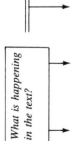

THE TEXT

Linda Partridge, 'Habitat Selection', in *Behavioural Ecology*, (ed. Krebs and Davies), Blackwell, 1978

apparently do not (Willson 1969, Soulé and Stewart 1970). There are of course formidable problems in making an adequate test of the hypothesis. It would be necessary to compare members of the same species from different areas or of different species, to demonstrate that habitat use was wider in some areas or species, and then to show that some character of importance in exploiting the habitat was more variable in the areas or species where the habitat use was broader.

There is one beautiful example where these rigorous demands have been met. Grant *et al.* (1976) have compared the medium billed ground finch (*Geospiza fortis*) on the Galapagos islands of Daphne and Santa Cruz. Bill size is more variable on Santa Cruz than on Daphne, and associated with this the finches occupy a much wider range of habitats on Santa Cruz. Grant *et al.* were able to show that on Santa Cruz shallow billed birds tended to inhabit parkland while deep billed forms lived in woodland. The deep billed birds were better at cracking large seeds than the small billed birds, and the latter cracked small seeds more efficiently. There was a higher proportion of large seed in the woodland habitat than in the parkland (see also 2.7).

What is happening in the text?

Which key words help us to understand what is happening in the text?

What is happening
in the text?

THE TEXT

Which key words help us
to understand what is
happening in the text?

Linda Partridge, 'Habitat Selection', in *Behavioural Ecology*, (ed. Krebs and Davies), Blackwell, 1978

Many ecologists believe that environments with high temporal heterogeneity will select for inhabitants with broad ecological niches (e.g. Levins 1968). Some evidence consistent with this view comes from the work of McDonald and Ayala (1974) who have shown that *Drosophila* populations kept in environments with high temporal heterogeneity in such factors as light, temperature and food show higher average heterozygosity than animals in less variable environments.

It has often been suggested that animals in the equable tropics face more constant environments than temperate animals. If this is true it follows that tropical animals should have narrower niches than their temperate counterparts. The same idea has been suggested for mainland as compared with island animals. These possibilities have been tested with respect to habitat preferences by Sheppard *et al.* (1968) and Klopfer (1967). Their results were inconclusive, and this aspect of the subject needs further study.

Appendix 6

Guide for Science students (for Chapter 9, exercise 2)

The following notes have been prepared by postgraduate students in Botany [at the Australian National University] to assist:

1 *potential* postgraduate students to finalize where, what and with whom they will study; and

2 *enrolled* postgraduate students to get the most value out of University-supervisor-student-project relationships.

The notes are intended to act as a general guide and are not intended as a substitute for other more detailed Faculty and Departmental documents.

Before committing yourself

1 Seek the best supervisor(s) for you and the project e.g. spend some time talking or working with potential supervisors and see how you relate on a day to day basis (personality clashes have caused problems in the past).

2 The supervisor(s) should actively be involved in the type of work you will be doing and have much of the equipment required.

3 Find out if the (main) supervisor has time-consuming commitments or plans to be away (on study leave, long service leave etc.) during the period of your study (especially during the early period and during the writing up period).

4 Two supervisors may be appointed: a primary supervisor and perhaps other supervisors or advisers. They will accept various responsibilities with respect to you and the project.

5 Approval to work for long periods in the field, or in another institution can be obtained, but is not encouraged by the University. It will be important to seek written permission from the Dean of the Faculty if this is to be at all substantial.

6 Be sure to clarify the expected extent of time, the availability of equipment and costs of travel or equipment. (It is not unreasonable for you to seek assurances on points 5 and 6, or to ask to

discuss aspects of them with anyone else who is likely to be involved, e.g. the 'owner' of equipment to which you will need access.)

7 Examine how soon you might reasonably expect to obtain experimental results, i.e. the time-scale of experiments and the time needed to master techniques before commencing.

8 Check with the supervisor and University on such requirements as course work, reports, seminars, demonstrating, obtaining assistance for research, conferences etc. and extending your project.

When you commence

1 Accept from the start that it is mainly your responsibility to succeed in your work. The supervisor is there to suggest, guide, help, criticize, advise, rather than to push.

2 Establish a good level of interaction with your supervisor(s) and members of this Department and related institutions. (Don't be put off if your supervisor appears busy.) Take every opportunity to mix and talk with other members of the department, whether it be at morning tea, seminars, meetings, or special functions. The department values this broader contribution from you, in addition to your special project work, and believes that this is a way in which you get much more from your time here than the specific research experience.

3 Commit your hypothesis to paper. This is part of the scientific method.

4 Lay out a plan to attack the problem.

As you proceed

1 A good relationship with your supervisor(s) is essential, and the basis of a good relationship is **communication**. Don't hesitate to take the initiative here. Seek out the supervisor with questions about the research area; put forward ideas for comment and criticism; voice worries while they are little ones rather than letting them grow, similarly with complaints; and as you start to collect results, make sure that you have discussions on these at an early opportunity.

2 Communication is not just oral. One of your main tasks will be to communicate your findings in writing. So as time goes on, practise communicating with your supervisor in writing — e.g. sets of results with a written interpretation and discussion — to get feedback not only about your work but your skill in communicating it. This will be invaluable when you get to the stage of putting together the final thesis.

3 Be prepared to modify your hypothesis and your experimental approach. You may need to call on expertise from elsewhere.

4 A worthwhile piece of research should end up in the form of a publication or two. The convention is that you would normally be senior author and the supervisor(s) junior author(s) on any papers based solely on your project work; but where there has been earlier research which led into it, unfinished work which is taken further by someone else, or parallel work which cross-links with yours, some different order of authorship might be appropriate and this kind of situation needs to be discussed openly and honestly to avoid misunderstanding.

5 If you find yourself in disagreement with your supervisor(s), don't worry about it for ages. Talk with your departmental committee representatives, head of department, or faculty student representatives, as necessary.